Academic VOCABULARY Toolkit

Mastering High-Use Words for Academic Achievement

Dr. Kate Kinsella

with Theresa Hancock

NATIONAL GEOGRAPHIC LEARNING | CENGAGE

Acknowledgments
Grateful acknowledgment is given to the authors, artists, photographers, museums, publishers, and agents for permission to reprint copyrighted material. Every effort has been made to secure the appropriate permission. If any omissions have been made or if corrections are required, please contact the Publisher.

Photographic Credits:
Wrap cover ©Victoria Ivanova/500px Prime.
Front cover (c) ©Yurchenko Yevhenii/Shutterstock
iv (tl) ©koya979/Shutterstock.com. (tr) ©monkeybusinessimages/iStock/Getty Images Plus/ Getty Images. (cl) ©Andersen Ross/Blend Images/ Getty Images. (br) ©KidStock/Blend Images/Getty Images.

Acknowledgments and credits continue on page 180.

For product information and technology assistance, contact us at
Customer & Sales Support, 888-915-3276

For permission to use material from this text or product, submit all requests online at **www.cengage.com/permissions**
Further permissions questions can be emailed to
permissionrequest@cengage.com

National Geographic Learning | Cengage Learning
1 Lower Ragsdale Drive
Building 1, Suite 200
Monterey, CA 93940

Cengage Learning is a leading provider of customized learning solutions with office locations around the globe, including Singapore, the United Kingdom, Australia, Mexico, Brazil, and Japan. Locate your local office at **www.cengage.com/global**.

Visit National Geographic Learning online at **NGL.Cengage.com**
Visit our corporate website at **www.cengage.com**

Printed in the USA.
Quad Graphics, Sussex, WI, USA

ISBN: 9781337296212

Printed in the United States of America
17 18 19 20 21 22 23 24 25 26
13 12 11 10 9 8 7 6 5 4 3 2 1

Contents at a Glance

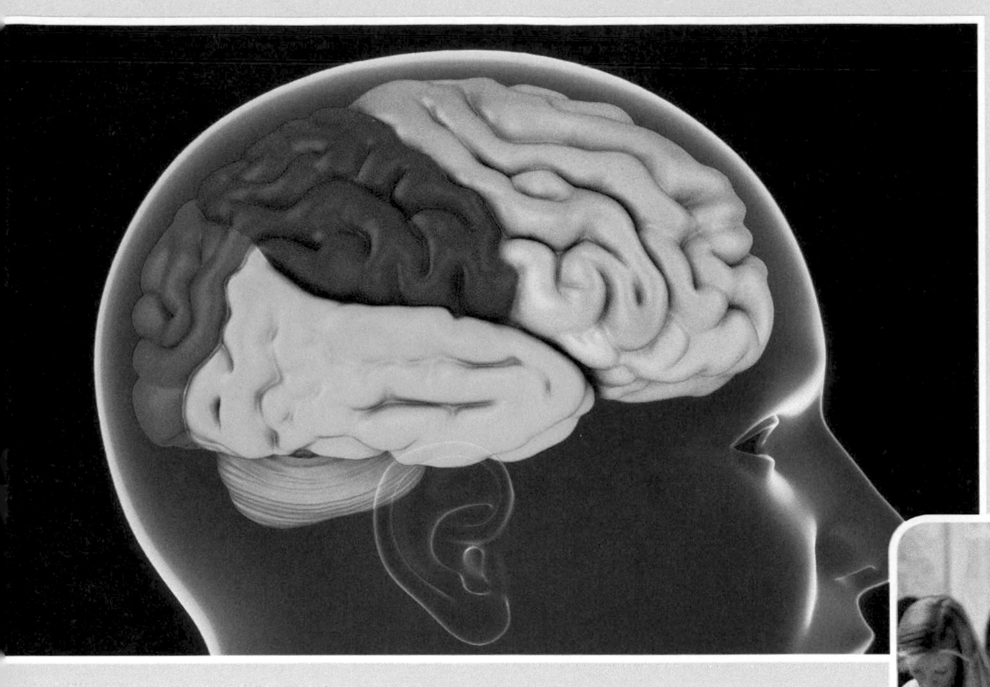

Unit 1
Describe

Unit 2
Analyze Informational Text

Unit 3
Cause and Effect

Unit 4
Sequence

ER SHALLOW
O NOT

Unit 5
Create

Unit 6
Compare and Contrast

Unit 7
Inference

Unit 8
Argument

Describe

To ***describe*** a person, explain how he or she looks, acts, and speaks. If possible, include what others think or say about the person.

To **describe** a location or a thing, use your senses to explain how it looks, feels, smells, sounds, and tastes.

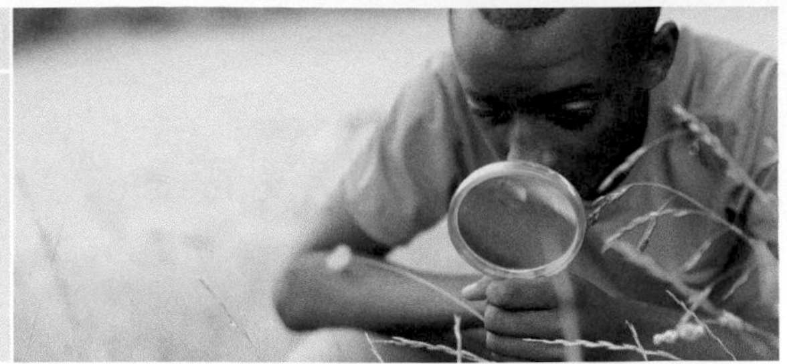

Find It

Read the sentences below and underline the words that describe a person, location, or thing.

1. My science teacher this year is amazing. Ms. Gomez is a tall and confident woman. She has a booming voice that is full of enthusiasm and excitement. She wears heavy, dark glasses which make her eyes look very big. She has a great sense of humor and often makes us laugh. At the same time, she is extremely demanding, and expects quality work from her students.

2. My father's apple pie is my favorite dessert. As it bakes, it has a delicious, comforting scent that fills our home. The first bite of the pie is the best. Its thick, golden, flaky crust melts in my mouth, and the flavor of the soft baked apples, oozing with sugar and cinnamon is incredible. My best friend says that it is the best pie she has ever eaten.

Try It

Think about one person you know. Write one important detail in each section of the chart that you would use to describe the person.

RATE WORD KNOWLEDGE

Rate how well you know Toolkit words you'll use to describe people, places, and things.

6th Grade	RATE IT: BEFORE	7th Grade	RATE IT: AFTER	8th Grade
characteristic	1 2 3 4	**explanation**	1 2 3 4	clarify
explanation	1 2 3 4	**respond**	1 2 3 4	symbolize
description	1 2 3 4	**unique**	1 2 3 4	function
accurate	1 2 3 4	**complex**	1 2 3 4	feature
demonstrate	1 2 3 4	**element**	1 2 3 4	coherent
feature	1 2 3 4	**attribute**	1 2 3 4	description

DISCUSSION GUIDE

- Form groups of four.
- Assign letters to each person.
- Each group member takes a turn leading a discussion.
- Prepare to report about one word.

A B
D C

DISCUSS WORDS

Discuss how well you know the seventh grade words. Then, report to the class how you rated each word.

GROUP LEADER Ask

So, ______________ (NAME) what do you know about the word ______________?

GROUP MEMBERS Discuss

1 = I **don't recognize** the word ______________.
I need to learn what it means.

2 = I **recognize** the word ______________,
but I need to learn the meaning.

3 = I'm **familiar** with the word ______________.
I think it means ______________.

4 = I **know** the word ______________.
It's a ______________ (PART OF SPEECH), and it means ______________.
Here is my example sentence: ______________.

REPORTER Report Word Knowledge

Our group gave the word ______________ a rating of ________ because ______________.

SET A GOAL AND REFLECT

First, set a vocabulary goal for this unit by selecting at least three words that you plan to thoroughly learn. At the end of the unit, return to this page and write a reflection about one word you have mastered.

GOAL

During this unit I plan to thoroughly learn the words ______________, ______________, and ______________. Increasing my word knowledge will help me speak and write effectively when I describe a person, location, or ________.

REFLECTION

As a result of this unit, I feel most confident about the word ______________.
This is my model sentence: ____.

explanation

noun

Say it: ex • pla • **na** • tion

 **Write it:** ______________ **Write it again:** ______________

 ______________

TOOLKIT

Meaning
a description or reason to make something easier to understand

Examples

- My brother's **explanation** for his missing ______________ convinced his teacher to extend the deadline.

- The history professor offered an **explanation** about the construction of The Great ______________.

Synonyms

- reasons

Forms

- **Singular:** explanation
- **Plural:** explanations

Family

- **Verb:** explain
- **Adjective:** explanatory

Word Partners

- (logical/reasonable) explanation
- (provide/offer) an explanation for

Examples

- There must be a **reasonable explanation** for why the gate was unlocked.
- The soccer coach insists that each player **provide an explanation for** an absence in advance.

 **Try It**

My coach asked me to provide an **explanation** for my missing ______________.

VERBAL PRACTICE

Talk about it **Discuss ideas with your partner, listen to classmates, and then write your favorite idea.**

Discuss
Listen
Write

1. One logical **explanation** for why the salad tasted terrible was that the chef may have added too (much/many) ______________ ______________.

2. My friend's **explanation** for why she is often late to school is that every day she has to ______________.

explanation

noun

WRITING PRACTICE

Collaborate

Discuss
Agree
Write
Listen

Discuss ideas with your partner and agree on the best words to complete the frame.

If you feel tired in the morning, a logical ______________ may be that you are not getting enough ______________.

Our Turn

Discuss
Listen
Write

Read the prompt. Work with the teacher to complete the frames. Write a thoughtful response that includes a convincing reason.

PROMPT: Imagine you offered to make posters for a school dance, but the class president declined. What are two reasonable explanations for the refusal?

If a chairperson declined my offer to make posters for a school dance, I think one reasonable ______________ for this could be that other volunteers had ______________ to promote the dance.

Another ______________ might be that the dance was ______________.

Be an Academic Author

Write
Discuss
Listen

Read the prompt and complete the frames. Strengthen your response with a relevant example.

PROMPT: Describe a time when you arrived very late to an important event. What explanation did you provide for being so late?

Once, I arrived very late for ______________.

The ______________ I provided for being so late was that my ______________.

Construct a Response

Write
Discuss
Listen

Read the prompt and brainstorm ideas for a thoughtful response. Construct a response that includes a convincing reason.

PROMPT: Describe a time that you felt extremely happy. What logical explanation can you offer for why you felt this way?

____

____

____

grammar tip

An **adjective** describes, or tells about, a noun. Usually an adjective goes before the noun it describes.

EXAMPLE: If you want to write an **interesting** essay, make sure you provide a **compelling** introduction and a **strong** conclusion.

respond

verb

Say it: re • **spond**

 ***Write it:*** ______________ ***Write it again:*** ______________

 ______________

TOOLKIT

Meaning

to reply or react because of something that has happened

Examples

When you receive a gift, it is polite to **respond** by saying, "______________".

Synonyms

- answer; reply; react

- After the team lost, the star player **responded** negatively by ______________ on the bench.

Forms

- **Present:**
  I/You/We/They respond
  He/She/It responds
- **Past:** responded

Family

- **Noun:** response
- **Adjective:** responsive

Word Partners

- fail to respond
- respond positively/negatively

Examples

- My sister **failed to respond** to the scholarship offer before the deadline.
- The school librarian **responded positively** to the news about a donation of hundreds of new books.

 **Try It**

It's usually a bad idea to fail to **respond** to (a/an) ____ ______________ from a teacher.

VERBAL PRACTICE

Talk about it

Discuss
Listen
Write

Discuss ideas with your partner, listen to classmates, and then write your favorite idea.

1. When a popular celebrity like ______________ appears on stage, the audience usually **responds** positively by clapping and cheering loudly.

2. When her mother asks her to ______________, my friend's little sister often **responds** negatively by complaining.

respond

verb

WRITING PRACTICE

Collaborate

Discuss
Agree
Write
Listen

Discuss ideas with your partner and agree on the best words to complete the frame.

It's generally annoying when some young children ______________________ negatively because they ______________________.

Our Turn

Discuss
Listen
Write

Read the prompt. Work with the teacher to complete the frames. Write a thoughtful response that includes a relevant example.

PROMPT: Imagine that someone said something negative about you to your best friend. How do you think your friend might respond?

If someone said something negative about me to my best friend, I'm ______________________ that my friend would ______________________ (positively/negatively). ______________________

For example, my best friend might say, "______________________ ______________________".

Be an Academic Author

Write
Discuss
Listen

Read the prompt and complete the frames. Strengthen your response with a personal experience.

PROMPT: Think about a recent invitation to attend an event that you received from a family member or a friend. How did you respond to the invitation?

Recently, I received an invitation from my ______________________ to go to (a/an) ______ ______________________. So I ______________________ (positively/negatively) ______________________ by ______________________ ______________________.

Construct a Response

Write
Discuss
Listen

Read the prompt and brainstorm ideas. Construct a thoughtful response that includes relevant examples.

PROMPT: Students respond to the stress of final exams in different ways. Describe how you generally respond to exam pressure, either positively or negatively.

____

____

____

grammar tip

An **adverb** that tells how many times something happens can go before or after a verb. The adverbs *always, usually, sometimes, often, frequently, typically,* and *never* generally go before the main verb.

EXAMPLE: I **usually** respond to an email right away. I **typically** answer the phone on the second ring.

unique

adjective

Say it: u • **nique**

 ***Write it:*** ______________________ ***Write it again:*** ______________________

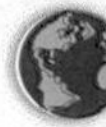 ______________________

TOOLKIT

Meaning	**Examples**
not like anything else	• No two ______________ are exactly alike; each one is **unique**. 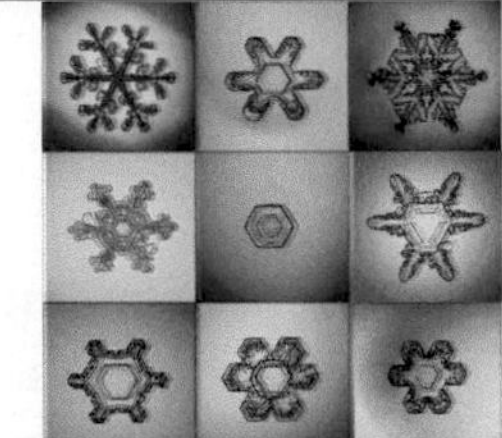
Synonyms • special; one-of-a-kind	• One **unique** feature of a giraffe is its long ______________. 

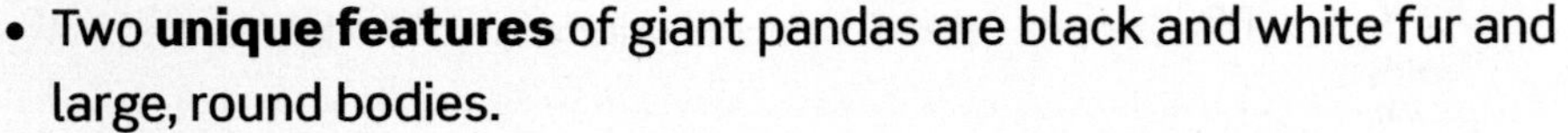

Family

- **Noun:** uniqueness
- **Adverb:** uniquely

Word Partners	**Examples**
• unique feature(s)	• Two **unique features** of giant pandas are black and white fur and large, round bodies.
• unique opportunity/ experience	• Performing in the Thanksgiving Day parade is a **unique opportunity** for our chorus.

 **Try It**

From my perspective, traveling to ______________________ for a study abroad program would be a **unique** experience.

VERBAL PRACTICE

Talk about it **Discuss ideas with your partner, listen to classmates, and then write your favorite idea.**

Discuss
Listen
Write

1. The singer ______________________ has such a **unique** voice that is easy to recognize.

2. One **unique** article of clothing that I own is my ______________________.

unique

adjective

WRITING PRACTICE

Collaborate

Discuss
Agree
Write
Listen

Discuss ideas with your partner and agree on the best words to complete the frame.

In our opinion, ______________________ are ________________ animals because they ____.

Our Turn

Discuss
Listen
Write

Read the prompt. Work with the teacher to complete the frames. Write a thoughtful response that includes a convincing reason.

PROMPT: Describe one unique experience that you would like to have in the future. Why?

One ______________________ experience that I would like to have in the future is to ____. One reason this experience would be unique is because I might see (a/an/the) __________________ ______________________________________.

Be an Academic Author

Write
Discuss
Listen

Read the prompt and complete the frames. Strengthen your response with a personal experience.

PROMPT: Describe one of the unique features that you've noticed about a cell phone.

One ______________________ feature I've noticed about about a cell phone is being able to ____. This was particularly helpful when I needed to ____________________________________ ____.

Construct a Response

Write
Discuss
Listen

Read the prompt and brainstorm ideas for a thoughtful response. Construct a response that includes a relevant example.

PROMPT: If you were asked to provide a brief positive description of the city or town in which you live, what unique features would you highlight?

____

____

____

grammar tip

Adjectives are always singular even if they describe a plural noun. Do not add **-s** to adjectives that describe plural nouns.

EXAMPLE: Several of our **new** neighbors have **furry** cats and **loud** dogs.

complex

adjective

Say it: com • **plex**

 ***Write it:*** ____________ ***Write it again:*** ____________

 ____________

TOOLKIT

Meaning

having many parts that are hard to understand

Examples

- The human ____________ is so **complex** we may never fully understand it.

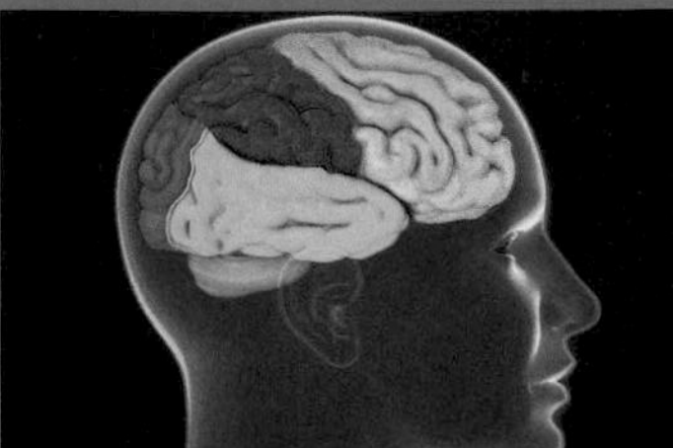

- Many people agree that ____________ is a **complex** issue.

Synonyms

- intricate; complicated

Antonyms

- simple; clear

Family

- **Noun:** complexity
- **Adverb:** complexly

Word Partners	Examples
• complex issue	• Climate change is a **complex issue** with no easy solutions.
• complex system	• My history teacher has a very **complex system** for grading papers.

 **Try It**

In my opinion, building (a/an) ____ ____________ seems very complex.

VERBAL PRACTICE

Talk about it

Discuss
Listen
Write

Discuss ideas with your partner, listen to classmates, and then write your favorite idea.

1. As you begin taking more advanced science classes, the ____________ ____________ become more **complex**.

2. An ecosystem, social networks, and a ____________ team are examples of **complex** systems.

complex

adjective

WRITING PRACTICE

Collaborate

Discuss
Agree
Write
Listen

Discuss ideas with your partner and agree on the best words to complete the frame.

In the workplace, schedules can become ______________ when several people ______________.

Our Turn

Discuss
Listen
Write

Read the prompt. Work with the teacher to complete the frames. Write a thoughtful response that includes a convincing reason.

PROMPT: Think about one of the complex issues that you would like to work at solving as an adult. Why is solving this issue important to you?

As an adult, I would like to work at solving a ______________ issue such as ______________. From my perspective, solving this issue is important because it would mean the end of ______________.

Be an Academic Author

Write
Discuss
Listen

Read the prompt and complete the frames. Strengthen your response with a relevant example.

PROMPT: Schools everywhere struggle with several issues, from retaining talented teachers to updating computer labs. Describe a complex issue that your classmates experience at your school.

At our school, one ______________ issue that we experience is the ______________. For example, ______________ which makes learning ______________.

Construct a Response

Write
Discuss
Listen

Read the prompt and brainstorm ideas for a thoughtful response. Construct a response that includes a relevant example.

PROMPT: Communities across the United States grapple with different issues, from inadequate affordable housing to outdated public transportation. Identify a complex issue that faces members of your community.

____

____

____

grammar tip

Adjectives are always singular even if they describe a plural noun. Do not add **-s** to adjectives that describe plural nouns.

EXAMPLE: My sister and I wore **wild** costumes and **crazy** shoes to my cousins' Halloween party.

element

noun

***Say it:* el • e • ment**

 ***Write it:*** ______________________ ***Write it again:*** ______________________

 ______________________

TOOLKIT

Meaning

a part or a small amount of something

Examples

- Exercise is an important **element** of any ______________ program.

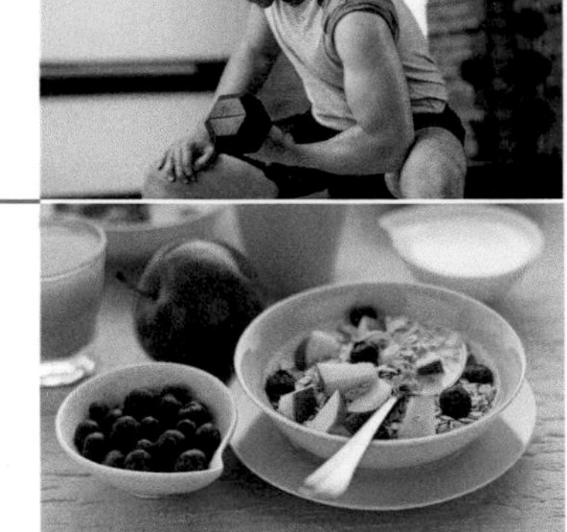

Synonyms

- part, component

- One key **element** of a healthy breakfast is including fresh ______________.

Forms

- **Singular:** element
- **Plural:** elements

Word Partners

- essential element
- key element

Examples

- Art and music are **essential elements** in the development of children.
- A **key element** of a good education is having teachers who believe in their students.

 **Try It**

At least one ______________________ is an essential **element** in a good playground.

VERBAL PRACTICE

Talk about it

Discuss
Listen
Write

Discuss ideas with your partner, listen to classmates, and then write your favorite idea.

1. The key **elements** of a good movie are a great story and ______________________.

2. If you want to learn the essential **elements** of a new language, the best way to start is to ______________________.

element

noun

WRITING PRACTICE

Collaborate

Discuss
Agree
Write
Listen

Discuss ideas with your partner and agree on the best words to complete the frame.

Polite communication and respect are both essential ____________ in building a strong relationship with (a/an) ______ ____________ at school.

Our Turn

Discuss
Listen
Write

Read the prompt. Work with the teacher to complete the frames. Write a thoughtful response that includes relevant examples.

PROMPT: Describe a group project that would be fun to accomplish at school. What key elements do group members need to have in order to complete the project?

When working on a group project, such as ____________, ____________ several key ____________ are needed in order to complete it.

For example, group members would need to have experience ____________ ____________ and skill ____________.

Be an Academic Author

Write
Discuss
Listen

Read the prompt and complete the frames. Strengthen your response with a convincing reason.

PROMPT: Who is your favorite musician? What is the key element that makes this musician unique?

My favorite musician is ____________. In my opinion, the key ____________ that makes (him/her) ____________ so unique is the way in which (he/she) ______ ____________.

Construct a Response

Write
Discuss
Listen

Read the prompt and brainstorm ideas for a thoughtful response. Construct a response that includes relevant examples.

PROMPT: It's easy to recognize a great story when you read one. What are some essential elements that you enjoy in a well-crafted story?

____

____

____

grammar tip

Quantity adjectives tell "how much" or "how many." Quantity adjectives go before a plural noun. Common quantity adjectives are: *most, many, some, several, both.*

EXAMPLE: Many students were interested in trying out for the school play, but **several** children had never performed in front of an audience before.

attribute

noun

Say it: at • tri • bute

 **Write it:** ______________ **Write it again:** ______________

 ______________

TOOLKIT

Meaning
a quality or feature of a person, place, or thing that is good or useful

Examples
- One essential **attribute** that ______________ need to possess is patience.

Synonyms
- quality; feature

- Three of Mary's many **attributes** include poise, confidence, and amazing ______________ talent.

Forms
- **Singular:** attribute
- **Plural:** attributes

Word Partners
- (a person's, place's, or thing's) many attributes include
- to have many (desirable/ admirable) attributes, such as

Examples
- **California's many attributes include** miles of beautiful beaches.
- The new school cafeteria seems **to have many desirable attributes, such as** large, clear windows, new, clean tables, and a huge salad bar.

 **Try It**
One of my bedroom's many **attributes** include (a/an) ______ ______________________.

VERBAL PRACTICE

Talk about it Discuss ideas with your partner, listen to classmates, and then write your favorite idea.

Discuss
Listen
Write

1. In order to become a great athlete you must have many admirable **attributes**, such as drive, focus, and ______________________.

2. One unique **attribute** of a computer is that it allows us to ______________________ ______________________.

attribute

noun

WRITING PRACTICE

Collaborate

Discuss
Agree
Write
Listen

Discuss ideas with your partner and agree on the best words to complete the frame.

If you want to learn how to ______________________, you need have many desirable ______________________, such as interest, discipline, and motivation.

Our Turn

Discuss
Listen
Write

Read the prompt. Work with the teacher to complete the frame. Write a thoughtful response that includes relevant examples.

PROMPT: What are desirable attributes a new community should have to attract home buyers?

In order to attract home buyers, a new community should have many desirable ______________.

For example, it should include ______________________, ______________________, and ______________________.

Be an Academic Author

Write
Discuss
Listen

Read the prompt and complete the frames. Strengthen your response with a convincing reason.

PROMPT: Think about a sport that you enjoy playing or watching. What are two attributes that an effective coach should possess?

Two important ______________ that an effective ______________________ coach should possess are compassion and a focus on ______________________. These are important because every player deserves ______________________.

Construct a Response

Write
Discuss
Listen

Read the prompt and brainstorm ideas. Construct a thoughtful response that includes relevant examples.

PROMPT: Many people would argue that teaching five-year-olds who are just starting school requires a very special person. What are the unique attributes of an effective kindergarten teacher?

____

____

____

grammar tip

The **preposition *to*** needs to be followed by a verb in the base form.

EXAMPLE: In order **to attend** college, it is crucial **to know** how **to read** and **to study**.

explanation

SMART START

explanation *noun*

DAY 1

My sister demanded that I provide an ______________________ for the mysterious damage to the ______________________ I had borrowed from her.

explanation *noun*

DAY 2

A logical ______________________ for why the kitchen table is wet is that someone ______________________________________.

DAY 3

There are several possible ______________________ for why your friend left the party early. For example, maybe she felt ______________________.

DAY 4

Our science teacher enhanced his ______________________ of how a steam engine works by showing us a ______________________.

DAY 5

When our flight was delayed for more than an hour, the ______________________ that the airline offered us was that they were experiencing ______________________ ______________________.

TOTAL

SMART START

REVIEW: explanation *noun*

DAY 1

No one in my family could offer a reasonable ______________ as to why there was (a/an) ______ ______________ in our living room. ☐ ☐

respond *verb*

DAY 2

When my friend failed to ______________ to my text message about getting together on Saturday, I felt extremely ______________. ☐ ☐

DAY 3

When students solve a difficult problem in class, the teacher usually ______________ by ______________. ☐ ☐

DAY 4

When my parents recently saw my ______________, they ______________ quite positively. ☐ ☐

DAY 5

When dogs feel happy, they often ______________ by ______________. ☐ ☐

TOTAL

unique

SMART START

REVIEW: respond *verb*

DAY 1

My friend's parents __________________ negatively when he asked them if he could ______________________________ .

unique *adjective*

DAY 2

Getting to meet and talk to (a/an) _____ ________________________ is one __________________ and exciting experience that every young person should have.

DAY 3

Our class field trip to __________________________ provided students with ___________ opportunities to learn about our rich local history.

DAY 4

One _________________ feature of my neighborhood is that we have (a/an) _____ ______________________________ .

DAY 5

Among my friends, I am __________________ because I have the ability to __________________________ .

TOTAL

SMARTSTART

REVIEW: unique *adjective*

DAY 1

The Spanish language is not ______________ to Spain. Many other countries, such as ______________, speak Spanish as their native language. ☐ ☐

complex *adjective*

DAY 2

The recipe for ______________ is quite ______________ because there are many ingredients and steps needed to make it. ☐ ☐

DAY 3

Middle schoolers have to navigate many ______________ social issues, such as learning how to be themselves and avoid ______________. ☐ ☐

DAY 4

(A/An) ______ ______________ is a ______________ system in which each individual has an important role in keeping everything running smoothly. ☐ ☐

DAY 5

As far as games go, ______________ is fairly ______________, so it takes time and effort to learn how to play it well. ☐ ☐

TOTAL

element

SMART START

REVIEW: complex *adjective*

DAY 1

When I need to solve a ______________ math problem, I usually try to ☐

____. ☐

element *noun*

DAY 2

In my opinion, a key ______________ of a perfect meal is an abundance of ☐

______________________. ☐

DAY 3

Trust and ______________ are two essential ______________ ☐

of a great friendship. ☐

DAY 4

When writing a research paper, a strong ______________ is an ☐

essential ______________. ☐

DAY 5

Perfect weather and a supply of snacks and drinks are some of the key ______________ ☐

for a successful and enjoyable ______________. ☐

TOTAL

attribute

SMART START

REVIEW: element *noun*

DAY 1

A key ______________________ of a successful video game is that it is ______________________ for the players. ☐ ☐

attribute *noun*

DAY 2

The President of the United States should possess several admirable ______________, such as courage and ______________________. ☐ ☐

DAY 3

When I shop for a new pair of pants, ______________________ is the most desirable ______________________ I'm looking for. ☐ ☐

DAY 4

In my opinion, one of the many positive ______________________ of my hometown is that it is very ______________________. ☐ ☐

DAY 5

Pet rabbits are usually ______________________, which is probably their best ______________________. ☐ ☐

TOTAL

Analyze Informational Text

Analyze means to carefully study.

Informational text can be found in many places, such as articles in a newspaper, magazine, textbook, or even on the Internet. **Informational text** provides important information about something and includes facts.

To **analyze informational text**, be sure to:

- read the title and headings
- read each section, paragraph, or list many times
- carefully study any pictures and charts
- discuss key ideas and important details
- think about what you've learned

Find It Read the sample texts below. Put a star next to the **informational text**.

The Light Catchers

by Allan Woodrow

The sky was dark, middle-of-the-night dark, even though it was only two hours past lunchtime. Why did they have to spend winter vacation with Grandpa Saul, anyway? If anyone asked Trevor for his opinion, he would have suggested they travel someplace far warmer, far brighter, and far closer. Nine-year-old Trevor and his eleven-year-old sister, Alice, flew on a plane for 13 hours to get all the way to their destination of Barrow, Alaska.

Seeing into Space

by Ray Villard

In 1609, a man named Galileo sat in his workshop, carefully grinding the lenses of a unique magnifying device. Unlike other such instruments, his "spyglass" would not be used for reading. The astronomer needed something to help him see into space.

Over four hundred years later, Galileo's spyglass, otherwise known as the telescope, has evolved into an important scientific tool. Telescopes allow us to peer across space and time into our vast, mysterious universe.

And no other telescope has affected this view more profoundly than the Hubble Space Telescope.

Try It **Analyze** the **informational text** by reading it several times. Then underline important details, and discuss what you learned using the sentence frames.

One fact I learned from the informational text is that telescopes ______________________.

Another fact that I learned from the informational text is that ______________________.

RATE WORD KNOWLEDGE

Rate how well you know Toolkit words you'll use to analyze text.

RATE IT

6th Grade	BEFORE	7th Grade	AFTER	8th Grade
analysis	1 2 3 4	**introduce**	1 2 3 4	interpret
position	1 2 3 4	**analyze**	1 2 3 4	critical
data	1 2 3 4	**consider**	1 2 3 4	investigate
evidence	1 2 3 4	**indicate**	1 2 3 4	factual
indicate	1 2 3 4	**objective**	1 2 3 4	present
concept	1 2 3 4	**subjective**	1 2 3 4	summarize

DISCUSSION GUIDE

- Form groups of four.
- Assign letters to each person.
- Each group member takes a turn leading a discussion.
- Prepare to report about one word.

A B
D C

DISCUSS WORDS

Discuss how well you know the seventh grade words. Then, report to the class how you rated each word.

GROUP LEADER

Ask

So, ______________ (NAME) what do you know about the word ______________ ?

GROUP MEMBERS

Discuss

1 = I **don't recognize** the word ______________ .
I need to learn what it means.

2 = I **recognize** the word ______________ ,
but I need to learn the meaning.

3 = I'm **familiar** with the word ______________ .
I think it means ______________ .

4 = I **know** the word ______________ .
It's a ______________ (PART OF SPEECH), and it means ______________ .
Here is my example sentence: ______________ .

REPORTER

Report Word Knowledge

Our group gave the word ______________ a rating of ________ because ______________ .

SET A GOAL AND REFLECT

First, set a vocabulary goal for this unit by selecting at least three words that you plan to thoroughly learn. At the end of the unit, return to this page and write a reflection about one word you have mastered.

GOAL

During this unit I plan to thoroughly learn the words ______________ , ______________ , and ______________ . Increasing my word knowledge will help me speak and write effectively when I analyze informational ______________ .

REFLECTION

As a result of this unit, I feel most confident about the word ______________ .
This is my model sentence: ______________________________
______________________________ .

introduce

verb

Say it: in • tro • **duce**

Write it: ____________________ ***Write it again:*** ____________________

____

TOOLKIT

Meaning

to meet a person or to present something to someone for the first time

Examples

- At Back-to-School Night, the principal **introduced** herself to my __________.

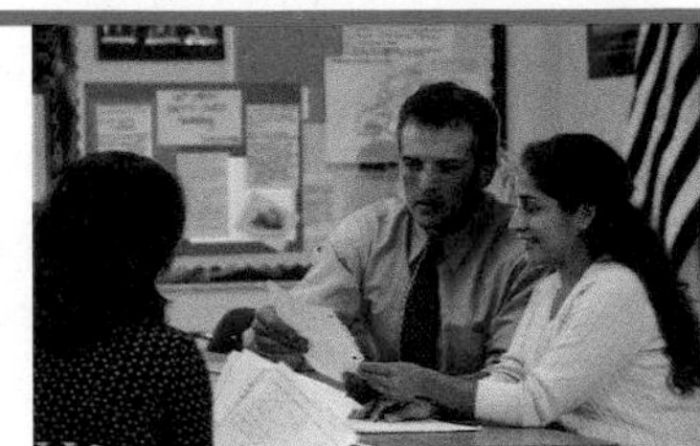

Synonyms

- show

- In the 1960's, companies **introduced** __________ with fluoride to reduce cavities.

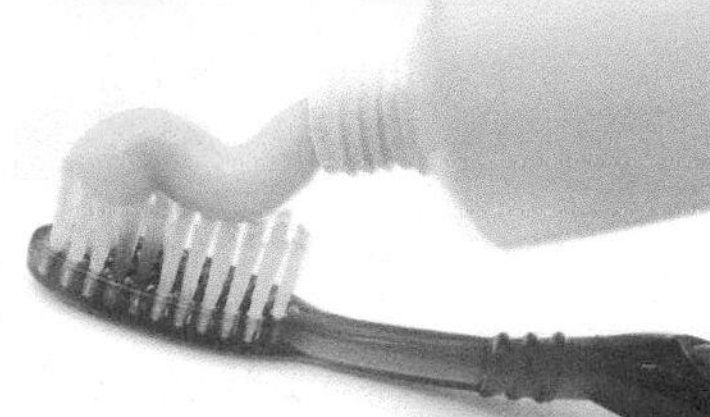

Forms

- **Present:**
  I/You/We/They introduce
  He/She/It introduces
- **Past:** introduced

Family

- **Noun:** introduction
- **Adjective:** introductory

Word Partners

- introduce a change
- attempt to introduce (something into /someone to)

Examples

- The chef will **introduce a change** to the cafe menu next month.
- The dance instructor **attempted to introduce a new step into** the routine, but it caused many students to fall.

Try It

My ______________________________ asked me to **introduce** a change in the practice schedule to my teammates.

VERBAL PRACTICE

Talk about it Discuss ideas with your partner, listen to classmates, and then write your favorite idea.

Discuss
Listen
Write

1. I would feel nervous but excited about being **introduced** to ____________________ ____________________.

2. It would be fantastic if our school **introduced** a change to the elective courses by offering a new class about ____________________.

introduce

verb

WRITING PRACTICE

Collaborate

Discuss
Agree
Write
Listen

Discuss ideas with your partner and agree on the best words to complete the frame.

A new item our cafeteria should attempt to ______________________ is ______________________ because they are ______________________.

Our Turn

Discuss
Listen
Write

Read the prompt. Work with the teacher to complete the frames. Write a thoughtful response that includes a relevant example.

PROMPT: Imagine you are planning a speech to become the president of a real or imaginary school club. Describe changes that you would introduce to make the club more enjoyable.

If I were planning a speech to become president of the ______________________ club, I would ______________________ changes to make it more enjoyable. For example, I would change the meeting time from Saturday mornings to ______________________ afternoons and offer awards to members who ______________________.

Be an Academic Author

Write
Discuss
Listen

Read the prompt and complete the frames. Strengthen your response with a personal experience.

PROMPT: Imagine that you had to provide a presentation about your favorite book or movie. Describe an exciting way you would attempt to introduce it to your classmates.

One way that I would attempt to ______________________ my classmates to my favorite (book/movie) ____________, ______________________, would be to create (a/an) ______ ______________________. I would include details about feeling ______________________ the first time I (saw/read) ____________ it.

Construct a Response

Write
Discuss
Listen

Read the prompt and brainstorm ideas for a thoughtful response. Construct a response that includes a personal experience.

PROMPT: Recall when a friend or family member introduced you to a particular sport or game for the first time. Describe your initial experience, including your performance and reactions.

____

____

____

grammar tip

Use **modal verbs**, or helping verbs, to give additional meaning to the main verb. Use *should* to make a suggestion or recommendation. Use *would* to show that something is possible under certain conditions. When you use a modal verb, add a verb in the base form.

EXAMPLES: We **should** eat less sugar. If we move to a house with a yard, I **would** like to have a dog.

analyze

verb

Say it: an • a • lyze

 ***Write it:*** ____________________ ***Write it again:*** ____________________

 ____________________

TOOLKIT

Meaning

to examine something in order to understand it

Examples

- If you **analyze** a person's __________, you can learn things about his or her personality.

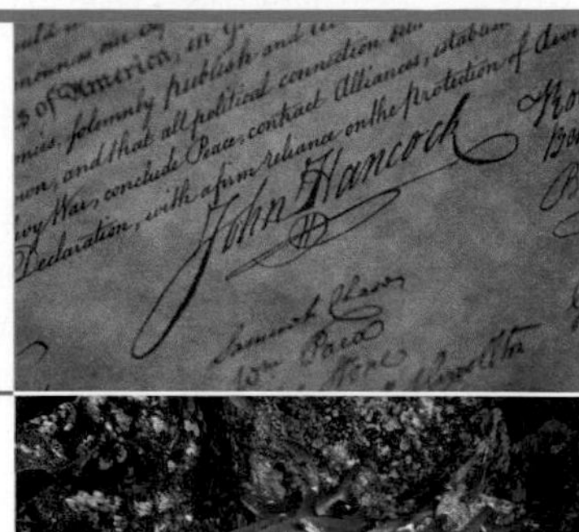

- Last summer, the marine biologist thoroughly **analyzed** many images to learn how __________ sleep.

Synonyms

- study

Forms

- **Present:**
  I/You/We/They analyze
  He/She/It analyzes
- **Past:** analyzed

Family

- **Nouns:** analysis, analyst
- **Adjective:** analytical

Word Partners

- carefully/thoroughly analyze
- to analyze the (problem/issue)

Examples

- To prepare for the competition, the debate team **thoroughly analyzed** arguments for and against a ban on plastic bags.
- The car mechanic had **to analyze the problem** with the engine before providing my father with the cost of the repair.

 **Try It**

A historian at a museum needs to thoroughly **analyze** ____________________ in order to understand the past.

VERBAL PRACTICE

Talk about it

Discuss
Listen
Write

Discuss ideas with your partner, listen to classmates, and then write your favorite idea.

1. Last year, I enjoyed the science unit where we **analyzed** the

____.

2. In the news this week, several reporters attempted to **analyze** the problems in

____.

analyze

verb

WRITING PRACTICE

Collaborate

Discuss
Agree
Write
Listen

Discuss ideas with your partner and agree on the best words to complete the frame.

During the science experiment, we examined a sample of ______________________ on a slide under a microscope to thoroughly ______________________ what was in it.

Our Turn

Discuss
Listen
Write

Read the prompt. Work with the teacher to complete the frames. Write a thoughtful response that includes a personal experience.

PROMPT: Describe a packaged snack that you used to think was a good choice, but which you learned is not healthy after carefully analyzing the nutrition information.

I used to think that ______________________ were a good snack choice. However, after I carefully ______________________ the nutrition label, I realized that this snack is not as healthy as I thought because it contains a lot of ______________________.

Be an Academic Author

Write
Discuss
Listen

Read the prompt and complete the frames. Strengthen your response with a relevant example.

PROMPT: The issue of whether zoos are beneficial or harmful for animals is controversial. What sources of information could you use to analyze the issue?

In order to ______________________ the issue of whether zoos are beneficial or harmful for animals, I could study several different sources of information. For example, I could read several articles from ______________________. I could also interview knowledgeable ______________________ and ______________________ to learn how animals such as ______________________ behave in a zoo and in the wild.

Construct a Response

Write
Discuss
Listen

Read the prompt and brainstorm ideas for a thoughtful response. Construct a response that includes relevant examples.

PROMPT: Should parents thoroughly analyze labels while purchasing groceries ? Identify ingredients contained in commonly eaten foods that parents should look for when making healthier food choices.

____

____

____

grammar tip

An **adverb** describes, or tells about, a verb. Adverbs usually end in *-ly*. Occasionally, adverbs come before the verb to describe how the action is done.

EXAMPLE: It is important to **carefully** review prior assignments before a test.

consider

verb

Say it: con • **si** • der

 ***Write it:*** ______________________ ***Write it again:*** ______________________

 ______________________

TOOLKIT

Meaning
to think about something or to have an opinion about something

Examples
- She **considered** ordering a ______________ for lunch, but she chose a salad instead.
- Many teens **consider** their parents' taste in ______________ to be old-fashioned.

Synonyms
- think

Forms
- **Present:**
  I/You/We/They consider
  He/She/It considers
- **Past:** considered

Family
- **Noun:** consideration

Word Partners
- carefully consider
- consider the possibilities

Examples
- Before casting a vote for the class president, you should **carefully consider** the attributes of each candidate.
- If you **consider the possibilities** of self-driving vehicles, it seems likely that several companies will pursue this technological advancement.

 **Try It**

When packing for a vacation, it is important to **consider** the ______________________________ ______________________.

VERBAL PRACTICE

Talk about it

Discuss
Listen
Write

Discuss ideas with your partner, listen to classmates, and then write your favorite idea.

1. I briefly **considered** purchasing (a/an) ______________________________ for my best friend's birthday, but I decided to get a more reasonable gift.

2. Many of my family members **consider** ______________________________ to be the best show on television.

consider

verb

WRITING PRACTICE

Collaborate
Discuss
Agree
Write
Listen

Discuss ideas with your partner and agree on the best words to complete the frame.

Before signing up for summer camp, you should ____________ the possibilities, such as seeing if engaging activities like ____________________ and ____________________ are available.

Our Turn
Discuss
Listen
Write

Read the prompt. Work with the teacher to complete the frames. Write a thoughtful response that includes a convincing reason.

PROMPT: Imagine two weekend activities that you would enjoy attending with friends. After carefully considering both options, which activity do you think your friends would enjoy more?

Two weekend activities my friends and I would enjoy are ____________________ ______________ and ____. After carefully ____________ both activities, I think my friends would enjoy the (first/second) __________ option more because ____.

Be an Academic Author
Write
Discuss
Listen

Read the prompt and complete the frames. Strengthen your response with a personal experience.

PROMPT: Think about a situation when you considered the possibilities of what might happen before taking action.

Once, when I had to ____, I ____________ the possibilities of what might happen before taking action. I thought about what would happen if I decided not to ____ ______________. Ultimately, I made the (right/wrong) ____________ decision because ____.

Construct a Response
Write
Discuss
Listen

Read the prompt and brainstorm ideas for a thoughtful response. Construct a response that includes convincing reasons.

PROMPT: Young people often have role models that some adults may not consider appropriate. Identify a famous person you admire despite this person's personal flaws or past mistakes.

____

____

____

grammar tip

An **adjective** describes, or tells about, a noun. Usually an adjective goes before the noun it describes.

EXAMPLE: It's not usually a **smart** idea to join friends in doing a **dangerous** activity.

indicate

verb

Say it: in • di • cate

 ***Write it:*** ______________________ ***Write it again:*** ______________________

 ______________________

TOOLKIT

Meaning

points to or shows that something is likely to be true

Examples

- When we went to the park, my sister's puffy eyes and runny nose **indicated** that she is ______________ to grass.

Synonyms

- point to; show

Examples

- Studies **indicate** that students who skip ______________ are more likely to be tired in class.

Forms

- **Present:**
  I/You/We/They indicate
  He/She/It indicates
- **Past:** indicated

Family

- **Nouns** indication, indicator
- **Adjective** indicative

Word Partners

- research indicates
- studies indicate

Examples

- **Research indicates** that girls have better fine motor skills than boys.
- Some **studies indicate** that exercising every day doesn't allow your body to heal and may actually cause muscle damage.

 **Try It**

Dogs **indicate** that they want to go for a walk by ______________________________.

VERBAL PRACTICE

Talk about it

Discuss
Listen
Write

Discuss ideas with your partner, listen to classmates, and then write your favorite idea.

1. Several studies **indicate** that texting while driving is ______________________.

2. The school survey results **indicated** that most students enjoyed the ______________________ last year.

indicate

verb

WRITING PRACTICE

Collaborate

Discuss
Agree
Write
Listen

Discuss ideas with your partner and agree on the best words to complete the frame.

During lunch, friends might ______________ that they have a seat for you by ______________.

Our Turn

Discuss
Listen
Write

Read the prompt. Work with the teacher to complete the frames. Write a thoughtful response that includes a convincing reason.

PROMPT: Research indicates that Americans are facing growing trends, such as poverty, educational disparity, and obesity. Describe one trend that you think needs to be addressed. Why?

Research ______________ that ______________ is a growing trend facing Americans. One reason that we need to ______________ this problem is because too many ______________.

Be an Academic Author

Write
Discuss
Listen

Read the prompt and complete the frames. Strengthen your response with a personal experience.

PROMPT: While tears often indicate that a person is unhappy, a person might also cry for other reasons. What is another reason a person might cry and what emotion might he/she be feeling?

While tears often ______________ that a person is unhappy, a person might cry for other reasons. For instance, I've seen my ______________ cry when (he/she) __________ was ______________.

Clearly, (he/she) __________ wasn't unhappy; (he/she) __________ actually felt ______________.

Construct a Response

Write
Discuss
Listen

Read the prompt and brainstorm ideas for a thoughtful response. Construct a response that includes a personal experience.

PROMPT: Many teachers provide feedback when grading reports and presentations by using a rubric. Describe what a recent rubric indicated about your performance on a particular assignment.

____

____

____

grammar tip

Use a **verb + ing** after the prepositions *by, of,* and *for.*

EXAMPLE: We bought a new leash **for walking** the dog. His unusual way **of barking** at the cat is disturbing the neighbors.

objective

adjective

Say it: ob • **jec** • tive

 ***Write it:*** ________________ ***Write it again:*** ________________

 ________________

TOOLKIT

Meaning

based on facts instead of feelings or opinions

Examples

- The teacher analyzed test scores and grades on homework in order to remain **objective** when preparing report __Cards__.
- Although she was a star player, the coach made an **objective** decision to cut her from the __Team__ for bad behavior.

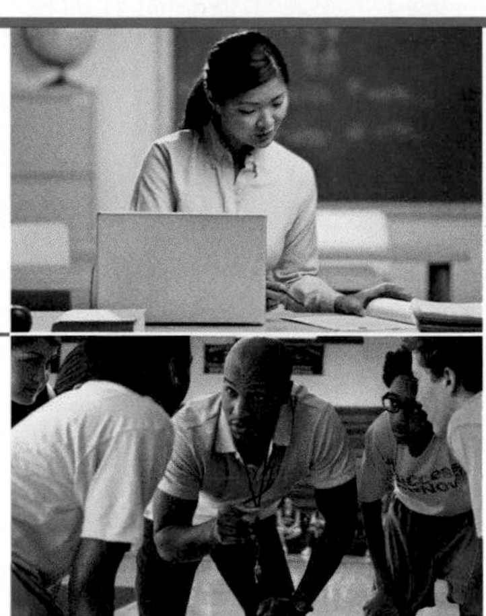

Synonyms

- fair; neutral; impartial

Antonym

- subjective

Family

- **Noun:** objectivity
- **Adverb:** objectively

Word Partners

- completely objective
- remain objective

Examples

- Supreme Court Justices should be **completely objective** when considering a case.
- The basketball coach **remained objective** when selecting starting players.

 **Try It**

When listening to friends arguing about what to ________________, I try to remain completely **objective**.

VERBAL PRACTICE

Talk about it — **Discuss ideas with your partner, listen to classmates, and then write your favorite idea.**

Discuss
Listen
Write

1. Sometimes it is difficult to remain **objective** about an issue, such as the ________________ ________________________________ ________________.

2. An **objective** review of my desk would reveal that I am (a/an) ________________ ________________________________.

objective

adjective

WRITING PRACTICE

Collaborate
Discuss
Agree
Write
Listen

Discuss ideas with your partner and agree on the best words to complete the frame.

One way to remain ____________________ when helping friends resolve a challenging problem is by ____ .

Our Turn
Discuss
Listen
Write

Read the prompt. Work with the teacher to complete the frames. Write a thoughtful response that includes a relevant example.

PROMPT: What resources would you carefully consider if you had to provide an objective report about a certain breed of cat or dog?

In order to provide an ________________ report about the ____________________ breed of (dogs/cats) ____________ , I would carefully consider several resources. For example, I would review articles from ______________________________________ with data that has been ______________________________ .

Be an Academic Author
Write
Discuss
Listen

Read the prompt and complete the frames. Strengthen your response with a relevant example.

PROMPT: Think about an activity that you feel strongly about, such as playing soccer or painting on canvas. Why it would be difficult to remain objective when discussing this activity?

I feel strongly about ____ .

When discussing this activity, it would be difficult to remain ________________ because I feel ____________________ and ____________________ whenever I think about it.

Construct a Response
Write
Discuss
Listen

Read the prompt and brainstorm ideas for a thoughtful response. Construct a response that includes a convincing reason.

PROMPT: Some teachers use a rubric to provide objective feedback and calculate a grade, while others make written comments and assign a letter grade. What approach do you prefer?

____

____

____

grammar tip

An **adjective** describes, or tells about, a noun. Usually an adjective goes before the noun it describes. An adjective sometimes appears after verbs such as *is, are, look, feel, smell,* and *taste.*

EXAMPLE: If you want to write a story that is **exciting**, make sure to include **interesting** characters and a **compelling** plot.

subjective

adjective

Say it: sub • **jec** • tive

Write it: ____________________ ***Write it again:*** ____________________

____

TOOLKIT

Meaning

based on personal feelings instead of facts

Examples

- Isabel's opinion of Mr. Arnold is **subjective** because he is her ____________ teacher.

Synonyms

- biased

Antonym

- objective

- The breakfast buffet includes many different ____________ because people's tastes are highly **subjective**.

Family

- **Adverb:** subjectively

Word Partners

- highly subjective
- is/seems subjective

Examples

- Taste in art is **highly subjective** because everyone has different feelings about what they see.
- My little brother is afraid of the dark, so his negative review of the scary television show **seems subjective**.

Try It

My opinion of ________________________________ is subjective because my family is from there.

VERBAL PRACTICE

Talk about it

Discuss
Listen
Write

Discuss ideas with your partner, listen to classmates, and then write your favorite idea.

1. My friends' opinions about the restaurant ________________________________ ____________ are highly **subjective** because it's their favorite place to eat.

2. The substitute teacher's **subjective** evaluation of our behavior was based on one small incident when a student forgot to ________________________________.

WRITING PRACTICE

Collaborate

Discuss
Agree
Write
Listen

Discuss ideas with your partner and agree on the best words to complete the frame.

Personal taste in clothing, such as wearing ______________________________,

is highly ______________________.

Our Turn

Discuss
Listen
Write

Read the prompt. Work with the teacher to complete the frames. Write a thoughtful response that includes a convincing reason.

PROMPT: Describe your favorite dessert. What makes your opinion about it highly subjective?

My favorite dessert is ______________________________ because

it tastes ______________________. The reason my opinion about it is highly

______________________ is because it is based upon my ______________________

feelings and tastes.

Be an Academic Author

Write
Discuss
Listen

Read the prompt and complete the frames. Strengthen your response with a personal experience.

PROMPT: Consider a time when you wanted to share a favorite movie, game, book or activity with a friend but they didn't seem interested. In retrospect, was your opinion subjective or objective? Why?

Once, I wanted to share ______________________________

with a friend, but (he/she) __________ wasn't interested. In retrospect, it's clear that my

opinion was highly ______________ because I felt so ______________________ about it.

Construct a Response

Write
Discuss
Listen

Read the prompt and brainstorm ideas for a thoughtful response. Construct a response that includes convincing reasons.

PROMPT: In the workplace, hiring decisions can be highly subjective. What are the benefits and disadvantages of companies not making more objective choices about new employees?

____

____

____

grammar tip

An **adverb** can describe, or tell about, a verb or an adjective. Adverbs usually end in ***-ly*** and come before the adjective to describe its quality.

EXAMPLE: My dog seems **strangely** upset about the new kitten.

introduce

REVIEW: attribute *noun*

DAY 1

When selecting applicants, colleges look for several desirable ______________ in students, such as ______________________________.

introduce *verb*

DAY 2

In order to improve my overall health and well-being, I will attempt to ______________ more ______________ into my daily routine.

DAY 3

One benefit to making friends from different cultures is that they can ______________ you to many interesting new ______________.

DAY 4

In order to reduce waste and become more eco-friendly, our school could ______________ some changes, such as ______________________________.

DAY 5

Our new ______________ recently ______________ herself to us.

TOTAL

SMART START

REVIEW: introduce *verb*

DAY 1

I was first ______________________ to classical music through

______________________ .

analyze *verb*

DAY 2

In order to ______________ the problem with our ______________________,

my mother had to spend an hour on the phone with customer service.

DAY 3

In language arts class last week, we ______________________ a famous

______________________ by looking at the language and symbols that the

author used.

DAY 4

While digging in the backyard, my uncle found some ______________________

that he thought might be old and valuable, so he took them to a museum to have an

archaeologist ______________________ them.

DAY 5

A professional therapist helps people to ______________________ their

problems and overcome difficulties, such as ______________________ .

TOTAL

consider

SMARTSTART

REVIEW: analyze *verb*

DAY 1

Detectives collect and ______________________ clues, such as ______________________, in order to solve mysteries.

consider *verb*

DAY 2

I generally ______________________ camping to be (a/an) ______________________ activity.

DAY 3

After ______________________ all of the possibilities for Saturday morning activities, my friend and I finally decided to ______________________.

DAY 4

Before choosing a new pair of shoes, you should carefully ______________________ whether they're truly ______________________ and how often you will actually wear them.

DAY 5

I have seriously ______________________ becoming (a/an) ______________________ after graduating from school because I think that would be an interesting and rewarding career.

TOTAL

REVIEW: consider *verb*

DAY 1

Before you participate in a dangerous sport, such as ______________________________ ______________, you should carefully ______________________________ what the consequences could be if something goes wrong.

indicate *verb*

DAY 2

Research ______________________________ that too much exposure to ______________________________ can be harmful for children.

DAY 3

Several studies have ______________________________ that increasing our consumption of ______________________________ can be beneficial for our health.

DAY 4

The baby's cries ______________ that she was ______________________________.

DAY 5

The grades on my current report card clearly ______________________________ that I have ______________________________ this year.

TOTAL

objective

SMART START

REVIEW: **indicate** *verb*

DAY 1

The weather reports I read yesterday ________________ that it would be ________________ on Saturday, so we should postpone our hike. ☐ ☐

objective *adjective*

DAY 2

When you give an ________________ analysis of an artwork, you should focus on the artist's ________________ rather than how you personally feel about it. ☐ ☐

DAY 3

It's important for journalists to remain as ________________ as possible when reporting on events such as (a/an) ________ ________________ ________________ and let the public form their own opinions about it. ☐ ☐

DAY 4

If I were to describe myself in a completely ________________ way, I would say that I am ________________. ☐ ☐

DAY 5

A purely ________________ description of a city would include basic information about its ________________. ☐ ☐

TOTAL

REVIEW: **objective** *adjective*

DAY 1

It's much easier to write an ______________ description of (a/an) ______ ______________ that you don't have an emotional connection to.

subjective *adjective*

DAY 2

Tastes in reading material are highly pleasant. For example, I love to read ______________, but most of my friends don't.

DAY 3

Many online articles seem quite ______________ because the authors use language that shows their ______________.

DAY 4

People's experiences of events are very ______________. For example, I had a fascinating time at (a/an) ______ ______________ while my friend was completely bored.

DAY 5

A friend's advice tends to be highly ______________. It can be helpful to seek advice from someone more neutral, such as (a/an) ______ ______________, when facing a complex issue.

TOTAL

Toolkit Unit 3 | Cause and Effect

Cause and Effect

A ***cause*** makes something happen.
Ask yourself, "Why did it happen?"
To find the **cause**, look for clue words such as *since*, *because*, and *reason*.

An ***effect*** is what happens.
Ask yourself, "What happened?"
To find the **effect**, look for clue words such as *so*, *as a result*, and *therefore*.

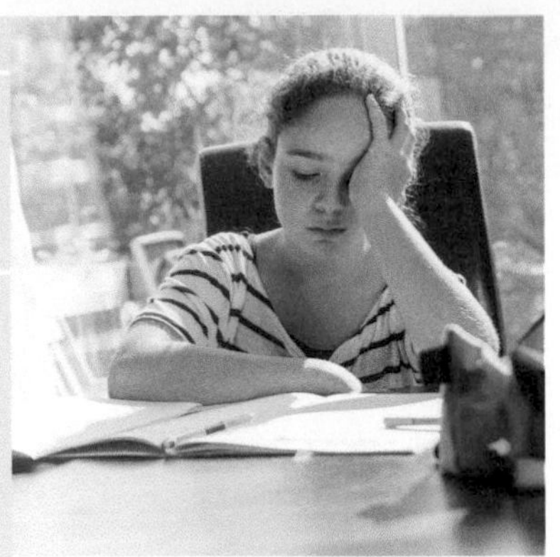

Find It **Read the sentences. Label the cause and the effect.**

I stayed up late studying. → I was exhausted in the morning.

Because I stayed up late studying, I was exhausted in the morning.

Cause — Effect

There was a powerful storm last night. → A few trees in the neighborhood fell over.

A few trees in the neighborhood fell over ***as a result of*** the powerful storm last night.

effect — cause

Try It **Complete the sentences. Then label the cause and the effect in each sentence.**

I lent my friend my Jacket since she was cold and I was not.

effect — Cause

I wasn't sure I understood the equation, so I asked my teacher for reteaching the lesson.

cause — effet

RATE WORD KNOWLEDGE

Rate how well you know Toolkit words you'll use to speak and write about cause and effect.

RATE IT

6th Grade	BEFORE	7th Grade	AFTER	8th Grade
influence	1 2 3 4	**significance**	1 2 3 4	alternative
reason	1 2 3 4	**reaction**	1 2 3 4	obstacle
cause	1 2 3 4	**various**	1 2 3 4	pattern
factor	1 2 3 4	**circumstance**	1 2 3 4	potential
lead	1 2 3 4	**influence**	1 2 3 4	trend
impact	1 2 3 4	**lead to**	1 2 3 4	resolution

DISCUSSION GUIDE

- Form groups of four.
- Assign letters to each person. A B D C
- Each group member takes a turn leading a discussion.
- Prepare to report about one word.

DISCUSS WORDS

Discuss how well you know the seventh grade words. Then, report to the class how you rated each word.

GROUP LEADER **Ask**

So, ________ (NAME) what do you know about the word ________?

GROUP MEMBERS **Discuss**

1 = I **don't recognize** the word ________.
I need to learn what it means.

2 = I **recognize** the word ________,
but I need to learn the meaning.

3 = I'm **familiar** with the word ________.
I think it means ________.

4 = I **know** the word ________.
It's a ________ (PART OF SPEECH), and it means ________.
Here is my example sentence: ________.

REPORTER **Report Word Knowledge**

Our group gave the word ________ a rating of ________ because ________.

SET A GOAL AND REFLECT

First, set a vocabulary goal for this unit by selecting at least three words that you plan to thoroughly learn. At the end of the unit, return to this page and write a reflection about one word you have mastered.

GOAL

During this unit I plan to thoroughly learn the words ________, ________, and ________. Increasing my word knowledge will help me speak and write effectively about cause and effect.

REFLECTION

As a result of this unit, I feel most confident about the word ________.
This is my model sentence: ________
________.

significance

noun

Say it: sig • **ni** • fi • cance

 ***Write it:*** ______________________ ***Write it again:*** ______________________

 ______________________

TOOLKIT

Meaning
being of great importance or value

Examples

- The Fourth of July has a lot of cultural **significance** for ______________.

- During the Olympics, seeing their country's participation has special **significance** to the team.

Synonyms

- importance; value

Antonyms

- insignificance

Forms

- **Singular:** significance
- **Plural:** significance

Family

- **Verb:** signify
- **Adjective:** significant
- **Adverb:** significantly

Word Partners

- explain the significance of (something)
- special significance

Examples

- Our teacher asked us to **explain the significance of** hip hop's influence on modern music.
- The color black has **special significance** during funerals in the United States.

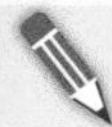 **Try It**

______________________ have special **significance** during a birthday party.

VERBAL PRACTICE

Talk about it Discuss ideas with your partner, listen to classmates, and then write your favorite idea.

Discuss
Listen
Write

1. The sport of ______________________ has a lot of **significance** at our school.

2. Our history teacher asked us to explain the **significance** of the ______________________.

significance

noun

WRITING PRACTICE

Collaborate

Discuss
Agree
Write
Listen

Discuss ideas with your partner and agree on the best words to complete the frame.

One movie that has a lot of significance to us is Titanic

because it has great actors.

Our Turn

Discuss
Listen
Write

Read the prompt. Work with the teacher to complete the frames. Write a thoughtful response that includes a convincing reason.

PROMPT: Describe a dish that has special significance to you. Why is it important?

A dish that has special significance to me is Duck Rice.

It is made with Fresh Duck. One reason it is remarkable is

because of its ~~flav~~ unique flavor.

Be an Academic Author

Write
Discuss
Listen

Read the prompt and complete the frames. Strengthen your response with a relevant example.

PROMPT: Describe an interesting location for field trip. Why would a visit to this place have special significance to you?

One interesting location for a field trip would be The White House

. Visiting this place would have special significance to me because

being able to go there

would help me understand how our president lives.

Construct a Response

Write
Discuss
Listen

Read the prompt and brainstorm ideas for a thoughtful response. Construct a response that includes relevant examples and a convincing reason.

PROMPT: Teenages often decorate their personal spaces with items that have special significance to them. Explain the significance of two items in your bedroom or locker.

Two things that have special significance to me are a picture of my childhood and a white metal box.

grammar tip

Noncount nouns name things that cannot be counted in English. Noncount nouns have the same form for "one" or "more than one." Do not add an **-s** to a noncount noun to make it plural.

EXAMPLE: This watch has personal **significance** to me. This **water** is frozen.

reaction

noun

Say it: re • **ac** • tion

 **Write it:** ____________ **Write it again:** ____________

 ____________

TOOLKIT

Meaning

what you say or do because of something that happens

Examples

- I was not surprised by my mother's negative **reaction** to the costly telephone ____________.

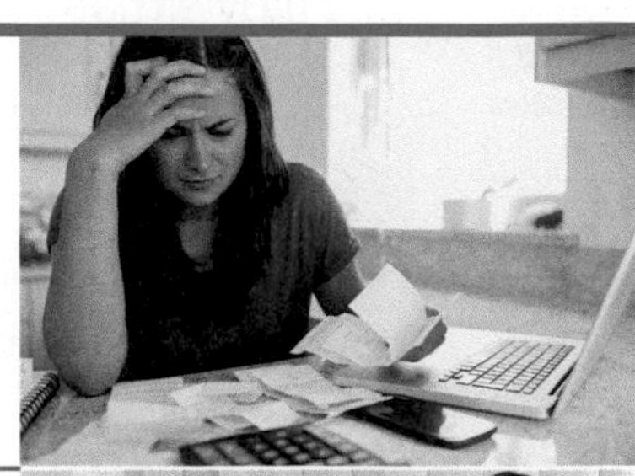

Synonyms

- response

- The children were excited when they saw their father's positive **reaction** to their new ____________.

Forms

- **Singular:** reaction
- **Plural:** reactions

Family

- **Verb:** react
- **Adjective:** reactive
- **Adverb:** reactively

Word Partners

- (immediate/initial) reaction
- (negative/positive) reaction to

Examples

- The little girl's **immediate reaction** after dropping her lollipop was to cry.
- Our entire class had a **negative reaction** to the news that the field trip was cancelled.

 **Try It**

If I heard that my best friend was moving away, my initial **reaction** would be to feel ____________.

VERBAL PRACTICE

Talk about it Discuss ideas with your partner, listen to classmates, and then write your favorite idea.

Discuss
Listen
Write

1. If I was unable to find my favorite ____________ my immediate **reaction** would be to search everywhere until I found it.

2. Many people have had positive **reactions** to ____________ ____________ new song.

reaction

noun

WRITING PRACTICE

Collaborate

Discuss
Agree
Write
Listen

Discuss ideas with your partner and agree on the best words to complete the frame.

On reality shows such as Dancing with Starts, people enjoy watching the contestants' emotional reaction to different challenges.

Our Turn

Discuss
Listen
Write

Read the prompt. Work with the teacher to complete the frames. Write a thoughtful response that includes a relevant example.

PROMPT: If you won a multi-million dollar lottery, what would your initial reaction be? What would you consider doing with some of the money?

If I won a multi-million dollar lottery, my initial reaction would be to cry ____________. I would consider using some of the money to buy a house for my all my brothers.

Be an Academic Author

Write
Discuss
Listen

Read the prompt and complete the frames. Strengthen your response with a convincing reason.

PROMPT: Think about a news report you have seen on television about natural disasters. Why do such events provoke emotional reactions among the public?

Natural disasters such as eartquake provoke emotional reaction among the public. One reason is that news programs usually show vivid scenery of people affected by the disaster. It is shocking to see victims who have lost their belongings, but it often causes people to help each other in unexpected ways.

Construct a Response

Write
Discuss
Listen

Read the prompt and brainstorm ideas for a thoughtful response. Construct a response that includes a personal experience.

PROMPT: Witnessing anyone being picked on at school is a challenging situation. Describe your immediate reaction after viewing a younger or smaller student being verbally or physically bullied.

My immediate reaction after viewing a younger studats beiny verbally bullied was to inform my teacher.

grammar tip

Count nouns name things that can be counted. Count nouns have two forms, singular and plural. To make most count nouns plural, add **-s**. To make count nouns that end in *x*, *ch*, *sh*, *ss*, and *z* plural, add ***-es***.

EXAMPLE: When my **brothers** helped us pack up the kitchen, they dropped two **boxes** of **dishes**.

various

adjective

***Say it:* var • i • ous**

Write it: ____________ ***Write it again:*** ____________

 ____________

TOOLKIT

Meaning

several different

Examples

- There were **various** road ____________ near the construction site.

Synonyms

- several; numerous

- My cousin offered **various** reasons for being late, but my uncle was still ____________ .

Family

- **Verb:** vary
- **Noun:** variety

Word Partners

- various reasons
- various factors

Examples

- The doctor determined that there were **various reasons** for my headaches, such as stress and dehydration.
- The firefighters discovered **various factors** that caused the fire.

 **Try It**

There are **various** reasons that people donate ____________ to homeless shelters.

VERBAL PRACTICE

Talk about it **Discuss ideas with your partner, listen to classmates, and then write your favorite idea.**

Discuss
Listen
Write

1. Teachers consider **various** factors like classroom participation and Homework when calculating grades for report cards.

2. We analyzed **various** factors in order to gather information for our research reports.

WRITING PRACTICE

Collaborate

Discuss
Agree
Write
Listen

Discuss ideas with your partner and agree on the best words to complete the frame.

There are Various factors to consider when adopting a pet, such as feeding, sheltering, and training.

Our Turn

Discuss
Listen
Write

Read the prompt. Work with the teacher to complete the frames. Write a thoughtful response that includes a personal experience.

PROMPT: Think of a recent time when you felt nervous about something you had to do. What were the various factors that contributed to your anxiety? What did you do to feel better?

Recently, I felt nervous when I had to perform on a Musical event.

The Various factors contributing to my anxiety were my fear of being on the stage and my uncertainty about the result. I tried to calm my nerves by taking a deep breath.

Be an Academic Author

Write
Discuss
Listen

Read the prompt and complete the frames. Strengthen your response with relevant examples.

PROMPT: Imagine that you had to decline an invitation to go somewhere with a friend. What are the various reasons you might offer to convey your regrets?

If a friend invited me to go to the concert, but I had to decline, I would offer Various reasons to convey my regrets. For example, I might say that I was already busy because I had to study, and that I also had to practice for the final examen.

Construct a Response

Write
Discuss
Listen

Read the prompt and brainstorm ideas for a thoughtful response. Construct a response that includes convincing reasons.

PROMPT: Identify a specific career that you might enjoy in the future. Describe the various reasons it reflects your personal values and interests.

One career that I might enjoy in the future is to become a teacher. My dedication and Patience are the varios reasons to pursue my career.

grammar tip

The **preposition to** needs to be followed by a verb in the base form.

EXAMPLE: Most teachers say that you need **to study** before an important test.

circumstance

noun

Say it: **cir** • cum • stance

 **Write it:** ____________________ **Write it again:** ____________________

 ____________________

TOOLKIT

Meaning

something that affects a situation

Examples

- Many people wondered what **circumstances** caused the people______ to abandon their house.

- The temperature is 109 degrees, so under the **circumstances**, the children cannot play______ outside.

Forms

- **Singular:** circumstance
- **Plural:** circumstances

Family

- **Adjective:** circumstantial
- **Adverb:** circumstantially

Word Partners	Examples
• in certain circumstances	• **In certain circumstances**, such as illness, it is possible for a student to make up an exam.
• under the circumstances	• Our star basketball player is injured, so **under the circumstances**, we are very happy to have won the game.

 **Try It**

I wasn't able to ______________________________ due to a special **circumstance**.

VERBAL PRACTICE

Talk about it **Discuss ideas with your partner, listen to classmates, and then write your favorite idea.**

Discuss
Listen
Write

1. In certain **circumstances**, like hearing a fire engine's siren, it might be acceptable for a driver to ______________________________.

2. The unusual **circumstance** that caused everyone to leave school early was the ______________________________.

circumstance

noun

WRITING PRACTICE

Collaborate

Discuss
Agree
Write
Listen

Discuss ideas with your partner and agree on the best words to complete the frame.

It's raining outside today, so under the circumstance we are unable to play soccer.

Our Turn

Discuss
Listen
Write

Read the prompt. Work with the teacher to complete the frame. Write a thoughtful response that includes a relevant example.

PROMPT: Imagine a cultural celebration where students share foods from around the world. Now, describe a circumstance in which not eating a certain food at the event would be acceptable.

At a cultural celebration, one circumstance in which not eating a certain food would be acceptable is when a student has (a/an) allergy ______________. For example, eating peanut butter or ______________, could be a problem for some students.

Be an Academic Author

Write
Discuss
Listen

Read the prompt and complete the frames. Strengthen your response with a relevant example.

PROMPT: Describe certain circumstances at a specific workplace environment that might indicate a gender or racial bias. What would you suggest to overcome this circumstance?

In a workplace environment, like (a/an) judicial department, certain circumstance that might indicate a (gender/racial) gender bias would be an unusually low number of females employees.

From my perspective, one way to overcome this is by encouraging the management to hire them. .

Construct a Response

Write
Discuss
Listen

Read the prompt and brainstorm ideas for a thoughtful response. Construct a response that includes relevant examples.

PROMPT: In certain circumstances, colleges and universities permit students to obtain an official work contract in order to miss classes for an entire week or more without penalty. From your perspective, under what circumstances should students be allowed to receive a work contract?

In certain circumstances, such as financial hardships, students should be allowed to receive a work contract.

grammar tip

Count nouns name things that can be counted. Count nouns have two forms, singular and plural. To make most count nouns plural, add **-s**. To make count nouns that end in *x*, *ch*, *sh*, *ss*, and *z*, plural, add **-es**.

EXAMPLE: Miss Simpson teaches art **classes.** I help her organize the **paints** and **easels**.

influence

verb

Say it: in • flu • ence

 ***Write it:*** ______________________ ***Write it again:*** ______________________

 ______________________

TOOLKIT

Meaning

to affect someone or something

Examples

- The weather report **influenced** our __________ for the weekend.

Synonyms

- change

- The advertisement strongly **influenced** her decision to try the new __________ .

Forms

- **Singular:**
  I/You/We/They influence
  He/She/It influences
- **Past:** influenced

Family

- **Noun:** influence
- **Adjective:** influential
- **Adverb:** influentially

Word Partners

- influence(s) behavior
- strongly/significantly influence

Examples

- People are not always aware of how advertising **influences behavior.**
- The author's personal life **significantly influenced** her novel.

 **Try It**

My teacher's encouragement strongly **influenced** my decision to write an essay about the issues surrounding ______________________________________ .

VERBAL PRACTICE

Talk about it Discuss ideas with your partner, listen to classmates, and then write your favorite idea.

Discuss
Listen
Write

1. Scientists are hopeful that recent media attention will **influence** politicians to dedicate funds toward finding a cure for Cancer ______________________ .

2. From my perspective, clasic music ______________________ **strongly influences** a student's ability to concentrate at school.

influence

verb

WRITING PRACTICE

Collaborate

Discuss
Agree
Write
Listen

Discuss ideas with your partner and agree on the best words to complete the frame.

In the last election, some politicians used social networks to influence voters' decisions.

Our Turn

Discuss
Listen
Write

Read the prompt. Work with the teacher to complete the frames. Write a thoughtful response that includes a personal experience.

PROMPT: Describe a recent occasion when a friend's encouragement about something strongly influenced your willingness to give it a try. What happened?

Recently, my friend's encouragement strongly influence my decision to try practicing writing. As a result, I tried it, and it turned out to be a (positive/negative) experience because I passed the writing test.

Be an Academic Author

Write
Discuss
Listen

Read the prompt and complete the frames. Strengthen your response with a personal experience.

PROMPT: Think about someone that you consider to be a positive role model in your life. Describe how this person influences your behavior.

One person I consider to be a positive role model in my life is Mrs. Gil. In particular, the way in which (he/she) She treats others with respect has influenced my behavior when I was her student.

Construct a Response

Write
Discuss
Listen

Read the prompt and brainstorm ideas for a thoughtful response. Construct a response that includes a personal experience.

PROMPT: Advertising in magazines, online, or on television can significantly influence a person's decisions. Describe an advertisement that significantly influenced your decision to purchase something. Did the item meet your expectations?

a shampoo advertisement that significantly influenced my decision to purchase a shampoo. After I tried it, I have noticed this product met my expectations

grammar tip

A **past-tense verb** describes an action that already happened. For verbs that end in silent ***e***, drop the final ***e*** before you add ***-ed***.

EXAMPLE: Last year, we **decided** to go to the beach. I **realized** that I **liked** swimming in the sea.

lead to

verb

Say it: lead to

 ***Write it:*** ______________ ***Write it again:*** ______________

 ______________

TOOLKIT

Meaning

to result in something or cause something to happen

Examples

- Eating a lot of chocolate before bedtime can **lead to** be awake.

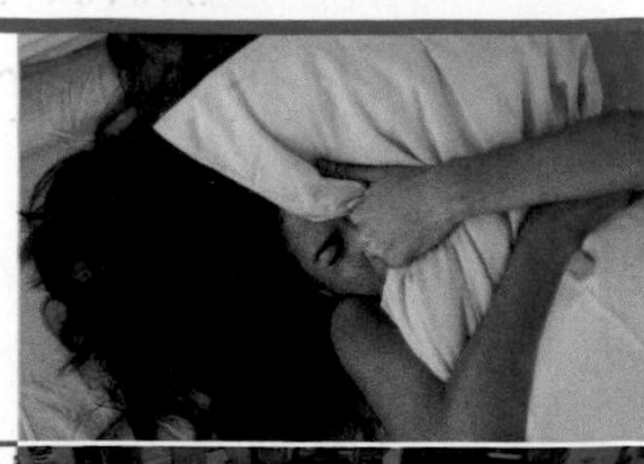

Synonyms

- cause

- An increase in Salary is likely to **lead to** the hiring of more teachers.

Forms

- **Singular:**
  They lead to
  It leads to
- **Past:** led to

Word Partners

- likely to lead to
- eventually lead to

Examples

- Taking your sister's jacket without asking her is **likely to lead to** an argument.
- If you leave the car's lights on, it will **eventually lead to** a dead battery.

 **Try It**

The new song 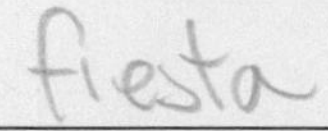 the fiesta ______________ is becoming so popular it is likely **to lead** to an increase in sales of the artist's new album.

VERBAL PRACTICE

Talk about it **Discuss ideas with your partner, listen to classmates, and then write your favorite idea.**

Discuss
Listen
Write

1. Community members are hopeful that the recent traffic incidents will eventually **lead to** the installation of a new  bump ______________ near the school.
2. Reading every night is likely to **lead to** (a/an) better ______________ vocabulary.

WRITING PRACTICE

Collaborate
Discuss
Agree
Write
Listen

Discuss ideas with your partner and agree on the best words to complete the frame.

A lack of exercise can eventually ___lead to___ problems with your ___health___.

Our Turn
Discuss
Listen
Write

Read the prompt. Work with the teacher to complete the frames. Write a thoughtful response that includes a personal experience.

PROMPT: Think about an incident when a particular type of communication, such as a note, text, or email, led to a misunderstanding. What happened and how did you correct the misunderstanding?

Once, I (sent/received) ______________ a/an ______ ___text message___ that ___lead to___ a misunderstanding. To correct it, I made sure to ___Clarify by sending a clear explanation,___ ______________.

Be an Academic Author
Write
Discuss
Listen

Read the prompt and complete the frames. Strengthen your response with a personal experience.

PROMPT: Who was the last person who gave you a compliment? What led to you receiving the compliment?

The last person who gave me a compliment was my ___Science teacher___ ______. In my experience, I believe my ___detailed notes___ ______________ (is/are) ________ what ___led to___ receiving the compliment.

Construct a Response
Write
Discuss
Listen

Read the prompt and brainstorm ideas for a thoughtful response. Construct a response that includes convincing reasons.

PROMPT: Group projects can provide opportunities for classmates to share creative abilities as well as the workload. Describe an experience where working as a team on an assignment did not necessarily lead to a positive final product.

Once, working as a team on an report, our disagreement on different points led to a failed score.

grammar tip

Use the **modal verb**, or helping verb, *can* to show that something is possible. When you use *can*, add a verb in the base form.

EXAMPLE: Students **can** enroll for extracurricular activities by filling in this form.

significance

SMART START

REVIEW: subjective ***adjective***

DAY 1

By nature, a persuasive essay is quite subjective, but it should still contain plenty of solid information to help convince the audience. ☐ ☐

significance ***noun***

DAY 2

An event of great historical significance that occurred in our state was the Gold Rush ______. ☐ ☐

DAY 3

The celebration of my mother's birthday has tremendous significance for my family. ☐ ☐

DAY 4

We rely on people who have studied History to explain the significance of many ancient texts. ☐ ☐

DAY 5

A past achievement that holds special significance for me was when I got my bachellor degree ten years ago. ☐ ☐

TOTAL

reaction

SMART START

REVIEW: significance *noun*

DAY 1

My grandfather asked me to explain the significance of the school event I included in my text message to him. ☐ ☐

reaction *noun*

DAY 2

When a coach or teacher criticizes my work, my initial reaction is to feel disappointment, but I understand that the critique will help me to improve. ☐ ☐

DAY 3

Almost everyone I know had a positive reaction to the movie Farenghelt. ☐ ☐

DAY 4

When I touch something extremely hot, my immediate reaction is to leave it. ☐ ☐

DAY 5

Once I tried to make a pie [illegible] for my family, but they all had very negative reaction when they tasted it. ☐ ☐

TOTAL

various

SMARTSTART

REVIEW: reaction ***noun***

DAY 1

When I came home late without calling my parents, their reaction was to scream at me without asking why of my lateness.

various ***adjective***

DAY 2

Various factors contributed to my low grade on the test, including my lack of confidence that week.

DAY 3

We bring various items with us to the beach, such as sunscreen, bathing suits, and (a/an) wide umbrella.

DAY 4

My friend and I get along extremely well for various reasons, such as our similar ideas about school.

DAY 5

I enjoy various types of music, including some metal music, which may surprise some people!

TOTAL

SMARTSTART

REVIEW: various *adjective*

DAY 1

A desire to help people in need is one of the various reasons that people choose to become an educator.

circumstance *noun*

DAY 2

Under no single circrumstance should any student behave Wrongly/inappro toward another student.

DAY 3

In certain Circumstance, such as on holiday weekdays, I am allowed to stay up very late.

DAY 4

There are very few circumstance under which I would eat Oysters, but my family loves them.

DAY 5

It's 96 degrees out today. Under the circumstance, we have decided to Stay at home.

TOTAL

influence

SMART START

REVIEW: circumstance *noun*

DAY 1

There are no eggs or milk in the refrigerator. Under the circumstance, we'll have to eat outside for breakfast.

influence *verb*

DAY 2

In moderation, video games can influence children positively by helping them develop other skills.

DAY 3

My mother has significantly influenced my taste in music.

DAY 4

Puppies can make great pets, but you'll probably need to use some strategies to support the dog's behavior.

DAY 5

The dark, cloudy sky strongly influenced our decision to go out last week.

TOTAL

SMART START

REVIEW: influence *verb*

DAY 1

My friend's tendency to get motion sickness strongly __influenced__ his decision not to go on the __movie__ with us last weekend. ☐ ☐

lead to *verb*

DAY 2

Participating in extracurricular activities, such as __sports__, often __lead to__ forming close and lasting friendships. ☐ ☐

DAY 3

I learned a hard lesson when my lack of preparation __lead to__ an embarrassingly poor performance during my __participation__. ☐ ☐

DAY 4

If we allow __forerng people__ to continue unchecked, it will likely __to lead to__ a huge global catastrophe in the future. ☐ ☐

DAY 5

A seemingly minor __symptom__ can sometimes __lead to__ a serious infection or illness. ☐ ☐

TOTAL

Toolkit Unit 4 | Sequence

Sequence

Sequence is the order in which events happen.

Use the signal words such as *first*, *next* and *last*, along with the Toolkit words in this unit to help you analyze, discuss, and write about the **sequence** of events.

Find It

Read the sentences. Determine the sequence and write **1st**, **2nd**, and **3rd** to show the order in which the events happen.

1. ______ I revised my thesis based on my partner's suggestions, and ended up with a greatly improved report.

   ______ The next day, my partner read the draft and made a lot of helpful suggestions.

   ______ Last week, I wrote the first draft of my science report.

2. ______ We took her home and named her Scout.

   ______ After visiting two shelters and seeing many different dogs, we fell in love with an energetic and affectionate two-year-old mixed breed dog.

   ______ About a year ago, my family decided to adopt a dog from a shelter.

Try It

Show the **sequence** by describing something that might occur after the first and second events.

1. Before going camping, you must make sure to pack all the camping gear you are likely to need.
2. After you get to the campsite, you should ______________________________.
3. Lastly, you will probably want to ______________________________ before you go to sleep.

RATE WORD KNOWLEDGE

Rate how well you know Toolkit words you'll use to speak and write about sequence.

RATE IT

6th Grade	BEFORE	7th Grade	AFTER	8th Grade
after	1 2 3 4	**requirement**	1 2 3 4	current
beforehand	1 2 3 4	**priority**	1 2 3 4	phase
subsequently	1 2 3 4	**initial**	1 2 3 4	transition
eventually	1 2 3 4	**series**	1 2 3 4	consequently
currently	1 2 3 4	**prior**	1 2 3 4	eventual
precede	1 2 3 4	**process**	1 2 3 4	ultimate

DISCUSSION GUIDE

- Form groups of four.
- Assign letters to each person. A B D C
- Each group member takes a turn leading a discussion.
- Prepare to report about one word.

DISCUSS WORDS

Discuss how well you know the seventh grade words. Then, report to the class how you rated each word.

GROUP LEADER Ask

So, ______ (NAME) what do you know about the word ______?

GROUP MEMBERS Discuss

1 = I **don't recognize** the word ______.
I need to learn what it means.

2 = I **recognize** the word ______,
but I need to learn the meaning.

3 = I'm **familiar** with the word ______.
I think it means ______.

4 = I **know** the word ______.
It's a ______ (PART OF SPEECH), and it means ______.
Here is my example sentence: ______.

REPORTER Report Word Knowledge

Our group gave the word ask a rating of 3 because I recognize the word but I need to learn the meaning

SET A GOAL AND REFLECT

First, set a vocabulary goal for this unit by selecting at least three words that you plan to thoroughly learn. At the end of the unit, return to this page and write a reflection about one word you have mastered.

GOAL

During this unit I plan to thoroughly learn the words lead to, ______, and ______. Increasing my word knowledge will help me speak and write effectively about ______.

REFLECTION

As a result of this unit, I feel most confident about the word ______.
This is my model sentence: ______
______.

requirement

noun

Say it: re • **quire** • ment

 ***Write it:*** requirement ***Write it again:*** ____________

 ____________

TOOLKIT

Meaning

something that you need or something that you have to do

Examples

- Wearing a glasses is a **requirement** if you want to play baseball or softball.

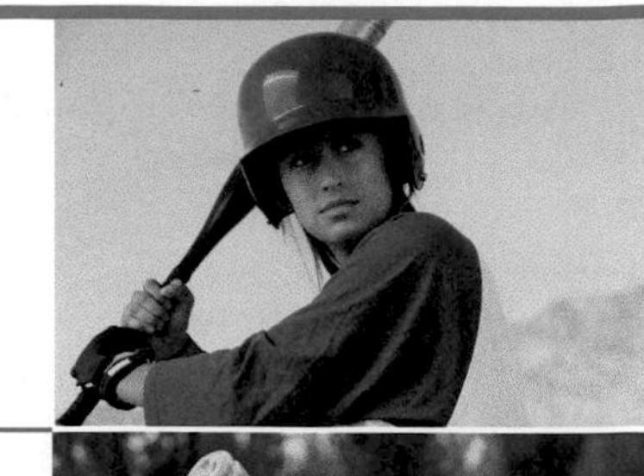

- Food and water are basic **requirements** that humans need to live.

Synonyms

- need; necessity

Forms

- **Singular:** requirement
- **Plural:** requirements

Family

- **Verb:** require
- **Adjective:** required

Word Partners

- meet (a, the, some, several) requirement(s)
- basic/minimum requirement

Examples

- In order to be accepted into the Language Academy, applicants had to **meet the requirement** of speaking at least three languages.
- Many modeling agencies now require runway models to meet a **minimum requirement** of being 6' or taller.

 **Try It**

To compete in an Olympic sport like soccer, athletes must meet several **requirements.**

VERBAL PRACTICE

Talk about it **Discuss ideas with your partner, listen to classmates, and then write your favorite idea.**

Discuss
Listen
Write

1. One of the main **requirements** for playing a school sport, such as basketball, is academic eligibility.

2. It is impossible to earn a good grade in biology class without meeting the minimum **requirements.**

requirement

noun

WRITING PRACTICE

Collaborate

Discuss
Agree
Write
Listen

Discuss ideas with your partner and agree on the best words to complete the frame.

The waste management agency has a minimum requirement for recycling, which includes sorting paper and metal items separately from all paper products.

Our Turn

Discuss
Listen
Write

Read the prompt. Work with the teacher to complete the frames. Write a thoughtful response that includes a personal experience.

PROMPT: Imagine your dream job. In your opinion, what are two requirements that you need to meet in order to pursue this career?

In my opinion, there are two requirements I need to meet in order to become a successful teacher. The first is to past various test. The second is to get a teacher credentials.

Be an Academic Author

Write
Discuss
Listen

Read the prompt and complete the frames. Strengthen your response with relevant examples.

PROMPT: If someone wants to become your best friend, what are a few of the minimum requirements that he or she would have to meet?

If someone wants to become my best friend, he or she would have to meet a few minimum requirements. In particular, that person would have to be respectful and willing to share his/her ideas.

Construct a Response

Write
Discuss
Listen

Read the prompt and brainstorm ideas for a thoughtful response. Construct a response that includes relevant examples.

PROMPT: Secondary school teachers tend to have strict requirements regarding due dates for major assignments. What do you consider to be fair requirements for late or incomplete work?

One fair requement for incomplete assigment could be to show what the reason is.

grammar tip

An **adjective** describes, or tells about, a noun. Usually an adjective goes before the noun it describes.

EXAMPLE: The **devoted** fans braved **miserable** weather to cheer on their team at the **first** game of the season.

priority

noun

Say it: pri • **or** • i • ty

 ***Write it:*** ______________ ***Write it again:*** ______________

 ______________

TOOLKIT

Meaning
the most important thing you have to do or give attention to before everything else

Examples

- On an airplane, ______________ is the top **priority**.

Synonyms

- importance

- Many parents place **priority** on doing ______________ before watching television.

Forms

- **Singular:** priority
- **Plural:** priorities

Family

- **Verb:** prioritize

Word Partners

- place priority on (something)
- give priority to (something)

Examples

- Our science teacher **places priority on** taking detailed notes during experiments.
- Congress's new budget **gives priority to** programs for education.

 **Try It**

My sister cares a lot about her grades, so studying her ___courses___ before a test is a high **priority** for her.

VERBAL PRACTICE

Talk about it **Discuss ideas with your partner, listen to classmates, and then write your favorite idea.**

Discuss
Listen
Write

1. Many ___managers in___ restaurants say that their top **priority** is to give customers delicious, authentic food.

2. Most teenagers give **priority** to their friends' opinions about ___music___.

priority

noun

WRITING PRACTICE

Collaborate

Discuss
Agree
Write
Listen

Discuss ideas with your partner and agree on the best words to complete the frame.

One way we can place priority on cleaning up our school campus is by encouraging students to bring reusable water bottles. reeyding all papers. reducing the use of plastic bottles.

Our Turn

Discuss
Listen
Write

Read the prompt. Work with the teacher to complete the frames. Write a thoughtful response that includes a convincing reason.

PROMPT: Imagine that you have to move to a new town or city. What would be a high priority for you?

If I had to move to a new town or city, finding (a/an) appartment would be a high priorty for me. One reason I would give priority to this task is that quiet neighborhoods mean a lot to me.

Be an Academic Author

Write
Discuss
Listen

Read the prompt and complete the frames. Strengthen your response with a convincing reason.

PROMPT: Imagine you and your classmates are planning a debate about an issue that many teens are concerned about. What topic would you give priority to discussing?

If my classmates and I were planning a debate, one topic I would give ~~to~~ priority to discussing is ~~bullying at school~~ gender equality global warming racial bias. I believe this is an important topic because I am very worried on how & concerned about my chances to get a job. disturbed about melting glaciers

Construct a Response

Write
Discuss
Listen

Read the prompt and brainstorm ideas for a thoughtful response. Construct a response that includes convincing reasons.

PROMPT: At age sixteen, teenagers in the United States can legally apply for a part-time job. What will be your two top priorities when seeking a weekend or summer job to earn an income?

In the United States teenagers can legally apply for a part-time job. My two top priority for seeking a weekend job to earn an income are at the Food Stores and a puble library.

grammar tip

Use the **modal verb,** or helping verb, *can* to show that something is possible. When you use *can,* add a verb in the base form.

EXAMPLE: Residents **can** leave their recycling in bins in front of their homes, or they **can** drop off their recycling at the recycling center.

initial

adjective

Say it: in • **i** • tial

Write it: ______________ ***Write it again:*** ______________

 ______________

TOOLKIT

Meaning

happening at the beginning of a plan, process, or situation

Examples

- Referees use a whistle to provide **initial** signals about fouls in a ______________ game.

- The **initial** step in the science ______________ is to carefully measure the liquid.

Synonyms

- first

Antonyms

- last; final

Family

- **Adverb:** initially

Word Partners

- initial phase/step/stage
- initial reaction/response

Examples

- The **initial step** in doing the laundry is sorting the clothes by color.
- When the undefeated soccer team lost their first game, the crowd's **initial reactions** were shock and disbelief.

 **Try It**

During the **initial** stage of preschool, many young children tend to cry ______________.

VERBAL PRACTICE

Talk about it **Discuss ideas with your partner, listen to classmates, and then write your favorite idea.**

Discuss
Listen
Write

1. The **initial** step in my process for getting ready for bed is to drink herbal tea ______________.

2. When my best friend recommended that I watch the new music video by ______________ Youtube ______________, my **initial** reaction was astonishment.

initial

adjective

WRITING PRACTICE

Collaborate
Discuss
Agree
Write
Listen

Discuss ideas with your partner and agree on the best words to complete the frame.

When preparing for (a/an) ___final___ exam, the ___initial___ step I take is to carefully organize my notes.

Our Turn
Discuss
Listen
Write

Read the prompt. Work with the teacher to complete the frames. Write a thoughtful response that includes a convincing reason.

PROMPT: Imagine you were asked to interview your favorite movie celebrity. What is the initial question you will include in your interview? What is the reason for asking about this topic?

If I were asked to interview my favorite celebrity, my ___initial___ question would be about (his/her) ___child hood___. The reason for asking about this topic is that I think it would reveal a lot about why (he/she) ______ selects roles that are so ___challenging.___.

Be an Academic Author
Write
Discuss
Listen

Read the prompt and complete the frames. Strengthen your response with a convincing reason.

PROMPT: Think about your initial reaction to a character in a novel or story that changed as you read the book or the series. What happened that caused your perspective to change?

When I began reading about ___heroes___ in the (book/series) ___history book___, my ___initial___ reaction was ___surprised/dislike___. However, when (he/she) ______ ___they showed their courage___, my reaction changed, and I began to think (he/she) ___they were___ was really ___~~heroes~~ caring or smart___.

Construct a Response
Write
Discuss
Listen

Read the prompt and brainstorm ideas for a thoughtful response. Include a convincing reason to strengthen your response.

PROMPT: Imagine you want ask to a parent/caregiver for a new pet. What do you think his or her initial response will be? What will you include in a letter to convince him or her to allow you to get it?

If I were asked to my parent a new pet, their first initial response would be to deny it. However, when I promise them that I will assume all task, they accept my proposal of have a pet.

grammar tip

An **adjective** describes, or tells about, a noun. Usually an adjective goes before the noun it describes.

EXAMPLE: The **following** paragraphs include **detailed** information about several **interesting** characters.

series

noun

***Say it:* ser • ies**

 ***Write it:*** ______________ ***Write it again:*** ______________

 ______________

TOOLKIT

Meaning

a group of similar things or events that follow each other in order

Examples

- This computer may look expensive, but it is the ______ one in the **series**.

- During P.E., we had to practice a **series** of steps for a difficult ______ routine.

Synonyms

- sequence

Forms

- **Singular:** series
- **Plural:** series

Family

- **Adjective:** serial
- **Adverb:** serially

Word Partners

- series of events
- series of steps

Examples

- In history, we learned about the **series of events** that led to the Civil War.
- The basketball coach asked one player to demonstrate the **series of steps** needed for a crossover dribble.

 **Try It**

The science fair judge complimented my 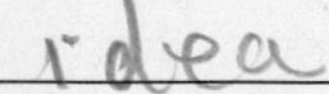 idea ______, but she suggested that I elaborate on the **series** of steps I took to accomplish the project.

VERBAL PRACTICE

Talk about it **Discuss ideas with your partner, listen to classmates, and then write your favorite idea.**

Discuss
Listen
Write

1. During eighth grade, we will have a **series** of events including (a/an) ______ zumba class ______.

2. My aunt asked my cousin to elaborate on the **series** of events that led up to the broken  window ______.

series

noun

WRITING PRACTICE

Collaborate

Discuss
Agree
Write
Listen

Discuss ideas with your partner and agree on the best words to complete the frame.

We enjoy watching several different series on television, including The Bing Bang Theory.

Our Turn

Discuss
Listen
Write

Read the prompt. Work with the teacher to complete the frames. Write a thoughtful response that includes relevant examples.

PROMPT: Certain holidays or celebrations are preceded by a series of events. Describe one holiday or celebration that you enjoy and name a few details in the series of events that lead up to it.

One (holiday/celebration) holiday that I enjoy is Christmas ________. There is a series of events that lead up to it, including a time when everyone Wraps presents, and another time when the family (gets/get) together to prepare traditional food..

Be an Academic Author

Write
Discuss
Listen

Read the prompt and complete the frames. Strengthen your response with personal experiences.

PROMPT: Describe the series of steps that you follow each morning to prepare to go to school.

Each morning, I follow a Series of steps to prepare to go to school. First, I take a shower, then I have a breakfast ________, and finally I go to school..

Construct a Response

Write
Discuss
Listen

Read the prompt and brainstorm ideas for a thoughtful response. Construct a response that includes relevant examples.

PROMPT: Think about your favorite book or movie. Imagine that your class is planning a series of events to celebrate the book or movie. What events would you suggest to your classmates?

____

____

____

grammar tip

Quantity adjectives tell "how much" or "how many." Quantity adjectives go before a plural noun. Common quantity adjectives are: *few, many, most, some, several, both.*

EXAMPLE: Many people play the lottery, but only very **few** people win.

prior

adjective

Say it: pri • or

Write it: ______________ **Write it again:** ______________

____

TOOLKIT

Meaning

happening earlier

Examples

- **Prior** to the start of the Olympic competitions, each team participates in the inaguration

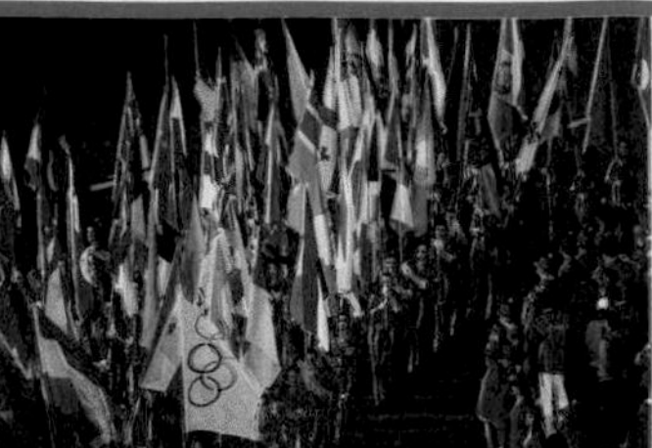

- The teacher had many years of **prior** experience.

Synonyms

- previous; past; earlier

Antonyms

- later; following

Family

- **Noun:** priority
- **Verb:** prioritize

Word Partners

- prior to
- prior experience/knowledge (of/about)

Examples

- **Prior to** the history test, we created a time line to review the series of events.
- When my bike's front wheel became stuck, I used my **prior knowledge about** gears and oil to fix it.

Try It

Prior to going to bed, I usually take a shower.

VERBAL PRACTICE

Talk about it Discuss ideas with your partner, listen to classmates, and then write your favorite idea.

Discuss
Listen
Write

1. In **prior** years, Sandy was a very popular song.

2. It would be impossible to get a job as (a/an) doctor assistant without any **prior** experience.

WRITING PRACTICE

Collaborate
Discuss
Agree
Write
Listen

Discuss ideas with your partner and agree on the best words to complete the frame.

The new history teacher has prior knowledge about the U.S. ~~History~~ Constitution because she worked as a researcher at the Smithsonian.

Our Turn
Discuss
Listen
Write

Read the prompt. Work with the teacher to complete the frames. Write a thoughtful response that includes a relevant example.

PROMPT: Imagine that you are planning a class party. There are several activities that the class will need to do to prepare. What are three things you and your classmates would do prior to the event?

Prior to a class party, there are several activities that need to be accomplished. First, we would make a list of games to play. Then we would plan what snacks to serve, such as pop corn. Finally, we would decorate the room with several balloons.

Be an Academic Author
Write
Discuss
Listen

Read the prompt and complete the frames. Strengthen your response with a personal experience.

PROMPT: Imagine that you are competing in the school science fair in a few weeks. What would you do prior to the competition? How did this help you in the past?

Two things I would do prior to competing in the school science fair are to decide a topic search for information and study the subject. This worked when I had an important presentation because it helped me feel more confident.

Construct a Response
Write
Discuss
Listen

Read the prompt brainstorm ideas for a thoughtful response. Include a relevant example to strengthen your response.

PROMPT: Describe a dream job that you would like to have someday, and discuss the prior knowledge or experience you would need to have in order to pursue such a career.

Prior to a dream job as a Writer, I have to take classes so I could acquire the needed knowledge how to write well.

grammar tip

A **past-tense verb** describes an action that already happened. To write the past tense, add ***-ed*** at the end of a verb.

EXAMPLE: Many years ago, we **moved** to San Francisco, and I **learned** to speak Spanish.

process

noun

Say it: pro • cess

Write it: ______________ ***Write it again:*** ______________

____

TOOLKIT

Meaning

a series of actions or changes that happen over time

Examples

- The **process** of getting a driver's ______________ usually includes taking a test.

Synonyms

- plan; sketch; drawing

- During the field trip, the guide described the complex **process** of painting the ______________.

Forms

- **Singular:** process
- **Past:** processes

Family

- **Verb:** process

Word Partners

- complex/simple process of
- a/the process for (doing a task)

Examples

- Learning how to fix a bicycle can be a **complex process of** understanding how different gears and components work.
- The substitute teacher asked us to describe **the process for** taking attendance.

Try It

My neighbor is trying to learn the complex **process** of  the entrance gate.

VERBAL PRACTICE

Talk about it

Discuss ideas with your partner, listen to classmates, and then write your favorite idea.

Discuss
Listen
Write

1. Some people learn how to write in Ingles ______________ easily, but for me it seems like a slow, complex **process**.

2. The simple **process** of learning how to write could ______________ can be challenging for many preschoolers.

process

noun

WRITING PRACTICE

Collaborate

Discuss
Agree
Write
Listen

Discuss ideas with your partner and agree on the best words to complete the frame.

In science class, we learned about the complex process of ~~working~~ water cycle.

Our Turn

Discuss
Listen
Write

Read the prompt. Work with the teacher to complete the frames. Write a thoughtful response that includes a convincing reason.

PROMPT: Describe a process for doing something at school that seems important to your teacher. Why is it important?

In our class, the process for following directions is important to our teacher. One reason is that when someone doesn't follow the process, the ~~teacher~~ student misses the recess time.

Be an Academic Author

Write
Discuss
Listen

Read the prompt and complete the frames. Strengthen your response with a relevant examples.

PROMPT: Think about a favorite meal. Is preparing it a simple or complex process? Describe some of the steps involved in the process of preparing it.

The (complex/simple) process of preparing my favorite dish, ceviche, involves several steps. The first step includes cutting a filet fish in small size.

I complete the process by ading lemon and salt.

Construct a Response

Write
Discuss
Listen

Read the prompt and brainstorm ideas for a thoughtful response. Include a relevant example to strengthen your response.

PROMPT: Imagine you are going to create an elaborate design for a car or a piece of furniture. Describe the steps you will take in the complex process of creating your design.

the complex process of creating a design for a piece of furniture, involves several steps. The first step i

grammar tip

Use a **verb + ing** after the prepositions *by, of,* and *for.*

EXAMPLE: The dancer overcame her fear **of performing by practicing** every day.

requirement

SMART START

REVIEW: lead to *verb*

DAY 1

The massive snowstorm last night led to the closing of several roads in our town.

requirement *noun*

DAY 2

Improving my grades is a requirement I need to meet before I'm allowed to get in the science department.

DAY 3

For a restaurant to receive a five-star rating from me, it would have to meet several requirements, the most important one being is to have beautiful place.

DAY 4

I believe a minimum requirement for being a police officer should be a sense of duty.

DAY 5

There are several requirement for getting a decent grade in my science class. One is that we must to complete the assignments.

TOTAL

SMARTSTART

REVIEW: requirement *noun*

DAY 1

One requequent for volunteering at the animal shelter is that you have to be responsable.

priority *noun*

DAY 2

In my free time, I give priority to my favorite activity, which is reading fiction. novel

DAY 3

When hiring temporary workers for the summer, some businesses give priorofy to young people who have less responsabilitu.

DAY 4

At home, my parents place a high priority on education ____________.

DAY 5

As a society, we spend too much time watching TV shows, when our ____________ should be to ____________.

TOTAL

initial

SMART START

REVIEW: priority *noun*

DAY 1

When I get home from a long day at school, my first priority is usually to take a rest.

initial *adjective*

DAY 2

During the initial days of the school year, we spend a lot of time reading books.

DAY 3

When people saw a working teenagers for the first time, I imagine their initial reaction was surprise and awe. sorpresa asombro

DAY 4

In the initial phases of learning how to exercise workout, you need to master simple exercises before you can perform more complex tasks.

DAY 5

When cleaning my room, my initial step is usually to pick papers up from the floor.

TOTAL

SMARTSTART

REVIEW: initial *adjective*

DAY 1

Sometimes your ~~Series~~ Initial impression of a person is not accurate. For example, you may think someone is Serious when actually that person is just very shy.

series *noun*

DAY 2

Each week we are given a serves of vocabulary words that we need to practice.

DAY 3

I enjoyed reading the entire series of fictional books.

DAY 4

Making a cake involves a long Series of steps, which ends with a party.

DAY 5

Near the beginning of one of my favorite movies, the main character ____________________, which touches off a long series of interesting events.

que da inicio a una larga serie de

TOTAL

prior

SMART START

REVIEW: series ***noun***

DAY 1

Late last night I heard a Series of strange noises, which turned out to be (a/an) a rat in the garbage can outside of our house.

resulto

prior ***adjective***

DAY 2

Prior to the 20th century, travel was much slower because people had to go by horse.

DAY 3

_______ to leaving on a trip, I make sure that I Wouldn't want to be at that time.

DAY 4

My prior knowledge about English Literacy led me to choose it as the topic of my oral report.

DAY 5

When I played basketball for the first time, I wasn't sure what to do, but my prior experience with similar games helped me figure it out quickly.

TOTAL

SMART START

REVIEW: prior *adjective*

DAY 1

I always prayed every night prior to going to bed.

process *noun*

DAY 2

At a summer camp, many children can learn the process of building tents.

DAY 3

The complex process of writing a report involves first doing research and then write a draft.

DAY 4

In math class, we just learned the process for adding variables.

DAY 5

Preparing pudin is a simple process. Boiling water is the hardest part!

TOTAL

Toolkit Unit 5 | Create

Create

Create means to make something.

To **create** a plan, solution, or an explanation you need to think carefully and consider different ways to answer a question.

To **create** stories, poems, and other pieces of writing you need to use your imagination and explore many ideas.

Find It

Read the sample tasks below and circle the steps that would help you create a strong response.

1. Think about the story of Cinderella and write a different ending.
   - a. Review the plot and think of ways for Cinderella to succeed without the Prince.
   - b. Change the setting to modern times.
   - c. Add a character based on yourself.

2. Explain how climate change is impacting the environment. Include two details to support your answer.
   - a. Think of two effects of climate change.
   - b. Find evidence that climate change is real.
   - c. Write about ways to reduce energy use.

Try It

Create a plan to convince your principal to start a school garden.

Reasons Why Our School Should ______________ a School Garden

1. Gardening can teach students life skills such as following steps.
2. Research shows that spending time outside can reduce the risk of diabetes.
3. Gardening can be used to teach many subjects such as biology.
4. Gardening can teach students about nutrition, which can help them avoid health problems such as obesity.

RATE WORD KNOWLEDGE

Rate how well you know Toolkit words you'll use to create plans, solutions, stories, poems, and other writing.

RATE IT

6th Grade	BEFORE	7th Grade	AFTER	8th Grade
approach	1 2 3 4	**contribution**	1 2 3 4	modify
generate	1 2 3 4	**develop**	1 2 3 4	communicate
include	1 2 3 4	**select**	1 2 3 4	organize
elaborate	1 2 3 4	**integrate**	1 2 3 4	preparation
plan	1 2 3 4	**solve**	1 2 3 4	option
design	1 2 3 4	**strategy**	1 2 3 4	solution

DISCUSSION GUIDE

- Form groups of four.
- Assign letters to each person.
- Each group member takes a turn leading a discussion.
- Prepare to report about one word.

A B
D C

DISCUSS WORDS

Discuss how well you know the seventh grade words. Then, report to the class how you rated each word.

GROUP LEADER Ask

So, ________ (NAME) what do you know about the word ________?

GROUP MEMBERS Discuss

1 = I **don't recognize** the word ________.
I need to learn what it means.

2 = I **recognize** the word ________,
but I need to learn the meaning.

3 = I'm **familiar** with the word ________.
I think it means ________.

4 = I **know** the word ________.
It's a ________ (PART OF SPEECH), and it means ________.
Here is my example sentence: ________.

REPORTER Report Word Knowledge

Our group gave the word ________ a rating of ________ because ________.

SET A GOAL AND REFLECT

First, set a vocabulary goal for this unit by selecting at least three words that you plan to thoroughly learn. At the end of the unit, return to this page and write a reflection about one word you have mastered.

GOAL

During this unit I plan to thoroughly learn the words ________, ________, and ________. Increasing my word knowledge will help me speak and write effectively when I create plans and ________.

REFLECTION

As a result of this unit, I feel most confident about the word ________.
This is my model sentence: ________
________.

contribution

noun

Say it: con • tri • **bu** • tion

 **Write it:** Contribution **Write it again:** ______

 ______

TOOLKIT

Meaning

something you do or say to help others

Synonyms

- addition; assistance; improvement

Examples

- Mario's **contribution** to the discussion helped us understand the subject.

- Rosa Parks made a major **contribution** to the Women Rights Movement.

Forms

- **Singular:** contribution
- **Plural:** contributions

Family

- **Verb:** contribute

Word Partners

- (major/significant) contribution
- (make/offer) a contribution (to/towards)

Examples

- Someday, I hope to make a **significant contribution** to the field of medicine.
- At the town hall, the mayoral candidate **made a contribution to** increase funding for the library.

 **Try It**

Our entire class gathered business`s people in order to make a **contribution** towards the local animal shelter.

VERBAL PRACTICE

Talk about it **Discuss ideas with your partner, listen to classmates, and then write your favorite idea.**

Discuss
Listen
Write

1. Cities often acknowledge people who have made significant **contributions** by naming their work after them.

2. The Pope Francasco has made a major **contribution** to world peace.

contribution

noun

WRITING PRACTICE

Collaborate

Discuss
Agree
Write
Listen

Discuss ideas with your partner and agree on the best words to complete the frame.

For the art show, the two best contributions were both sculptures/Murals made with polished bronze/recycled plastic

Our Turn

Discuss
Listen
Write

Read the prompt. Work with the teacher to complete the frames. Write a thoughtful response that includes a convincing reason.

PROMPT: Imagine you were asked to offer a contribution to the school newspaper describing an important issue affecting many teens. Why is it important to discuss this topic?

If I was asked to offer a contribution to the school newspaper I would describe the issue of ~~the children rights~~ depresion. One reason this is important to discuss is that so many unfair rules at home teens are soffering.

Be an Academic Author

Write
Discuss
Listen

Read the prompt and complete the frames. Strengthen your response with a personal experience.

PROMPT: Think about a social networking site or app that has made significant contributions to the ways in which people communicate. Has every interaction been entirely positive? Why or why not?

From my perspective, one social networking (site/app) ______ that has made significant contribution to the ways in which people communicate is Messenger ______. However, (not every/every) not every interaction has been entirely positive. For example, I know of some incidents when people got Stressed after so many calls.

Construct a Response

Write
Discuss
Listen

Read the prompt and brainstorm ideas for a thoughtful response. Construct a response that includes convincing reasons.

PROMPT: Describe someone who has made a significant contribution to you or to your community. Explain why their contribution made a positive impact on your life or where you live.

One who has made a scgnificant contribution in my life is my microbiology teacher. Her Care and support during a difficult time were the major effect on my decision to become a teacher.

grammar tip

Quantity adjectives tell "how much" or "how many." Quantity adjectives go before a plural noun. Common quantity adjectives are: *many, most, some, several, both.*

EXAMPLE: I have just one sister, but **many** people I know have **several** brothers.

develop

verb

Say it: de • **vel** • op

 ***Write it:*** ____________ ***Write it again:*** ____________

 ____________

TOOLKIT

Meaning
to begin; to change into something more

Examples
- A flood **developed** after several days of raining.

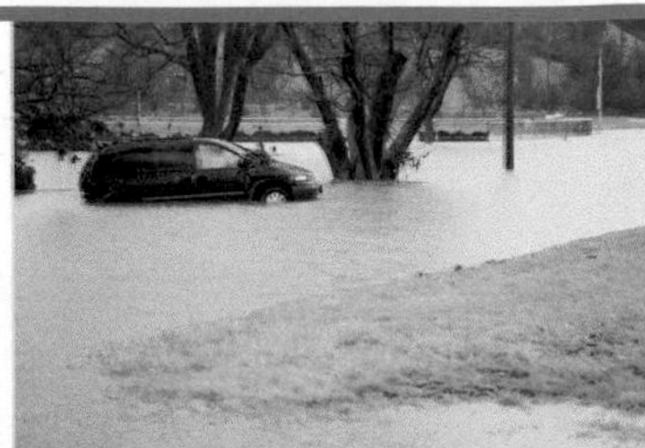

Synonyms
- start; grow; increase

- The coach was confident that the team would eventually **develop** skills needed to win the tournament.

Forms
- **Present:**
  I/You/We/They develop
  He/She/It develops
- **Past:** developed

Family
- **Noun:** development
- **Adjectives:** developed, developing, developmental

Word Partners
- develop skills
- develop the ability to do something

Examples
- An internship can help you **develop skills** in the workplace.
- After several hours of practice, my sister **developed the ability to do a handstand.**

 **Try It**

If you work hard, you can **develop** the ability to reach you goals.

VERBAL PRACTICE

Talk about it **Discuss ideas with your partner, listen to classmates, and then write your favorite idea.**

Discuss
Listen
Write

1. Watching cooking shows can help you **develop** skills to make interesting dishes like duck rice.

2. We worked in groups to **develop** a variety of ideas for the end-of-year in the school.

develop

verb

WRITING PRACTICE

Collaborate

Discuss
Agree
Write
Listen

Discuss ideas with your partner and agree on the best words to complete the frame.

The best way to handle a disagreement that has developed in class is to be respectful with other ideas.

Our Turn

Discuss
Listen
Write

Read the prompt. Work with the teacher to complete the frames. Write a thoughtful response that includes a relevant example.

PROMPT: Describe an activity, such as a hobby or sport, that you have developed your skills in over the past year. What are two things you did to improve?

Over the past year, I have developed my skills in writing.

In particular, I improved by practicung daily

and working hard to ______.

Be an Academic Author

Write
Discuss
Listen

Read the prompt and complete the frames. Strengthen your response with a convincing reason.

PROMPT: Describe a new technology that scientists might develop in the future that will allow people to do something that they are unable to do right now. How will this new technology help?

In the future, scientist might develop technology that allows people to fly. This technology would be particularly helpful because it would save time to go anywhere.

Construct a Response

Write
Discuss
Listen

Read the prompt and brainstorm ideas for a thoughtful response. Construct a response that includes relevant examples.

PROMPT: It takes considerable guidance and practice to develop the ability to compete as an Olympic athlete. Describe how athletes might develop their skills for a particular Olympic sport.

To Compete as a Olympic athlete, runners need to develop the ability to run faster.

grammar tip

The **present perfect tense** is formed with *has/have* + the **past participle** form of the verb. To write the past participle of a regular verb, use the base form of the verb plus ***-ed***. For verbs that end in silent ***e***, drop the final ***e*** before you add ***-ed***.

EXAMPLE: My sister **has received** a letter. She **has improved** her acting skills in the last year.

select

verb

Say it: se • **lect**

 ***Write it:*** ______________ ***Write it again:*** ______________

 ______________

TOOLKIT

Meaning

to choose

Examples

- My sister usually **selects** what she's going to __________ to school the night before.

- The little boy carefully **selected** the flavor of ice cream he wanted on his __________.

Synonyms

- pick

Forms

- **Present:**

I/You/We/They	select
He/She/It	selects

- **Past:** selected

Family

- **Noun:** selection
- **Adjective:** selective
- **Adverb:** selectively

Word Partners

- (carefully/randomly) select
- select the (option/type) of

Examples

- Researchers **randomly selected** 50 students to participate in the study.
- When purchasing a new computer, you can **select the option of** designing a custom case for it.

 **Try It**

The planning committee carefully **selected** the customs__________ for this year's dance.

VERBAL PRACTICE

Talk about it **Discuss ideas with your partner, listen to classmates, and then write your favorite idea.**

Discuss
Listen
Write

1. When ordering dessert, I usually **select** chocolate cake__________.
2. Last year, our teacher **selected** the old movie "Nana Mia"__________ __________ for us to watch in class.

select

verb

WRITING PRACTICE

Collaborate

Discuss
Agree
Write
Listen

Discuss ideas with your partner and agree on the best words to complete the frame.

Before you select a new ipad, it is important to conduct some research about it first.

Our Turn

Discuss
Listen
Write

Read the prompt. Work with the teacher to complete the frames. Write a thoughtful response that includes a convincing reason.

PROMPT: Describe a situation when a teacher, coach, or adult might randomly select a person to do a task. Why does this seem fair/unfair to you?

A Coach might randomly select a student when they want that person to compete in the sport event.

In my opinion, this seems (fair/unfair) fair because ~~each~~ all students posses the ability to get the prize.

Be an Academic Author

Write
Discuss
Listen

Read the prompt and complete the frames. Strengthen your response with a convincing reason.

PROMPT: Describe a time recently when a family member selected an option for a device purchased for your home. What option was selected, and was it a good or bad choice?

Recently, my brother purchased a/an new fan and Selected the option for a/an control remote. This option turned out to be a (good/bad) good choice because it is easier to turn it on.

Construct a Response

Write
Discuss
Listen

Read the prompt and brainstorm ideas for a thoughtful response. Construct a response that includes relevant examples.

PROMPT: Before purchasing a used car, there are many factors to consider, from maintenance costs to mileage. Identify three factors your family should contemplate before selecting a used car.

Before purchasing a used car, one should contemplate ~~select the~~ option of less mileage, appropriate condition, and reasonable price.

grammar tip

A **common noun** names a person, place, thing, or idea. **Singular nouns** name one person, place, thing, or idea. The words *a, an, one,* and *the* often appear before a singular noun.

EXAMPLE: One person will lead **the class** on **a nature walk.**

integrate

verb

Say it: in • te • grate

Write it: ______________________ ***Write it again:*** ______________________

____

TOOLKIT

Meaning

to bring different things or people together

Examples

- Many teachers work hard to **integrate** P. E. into their lessons.

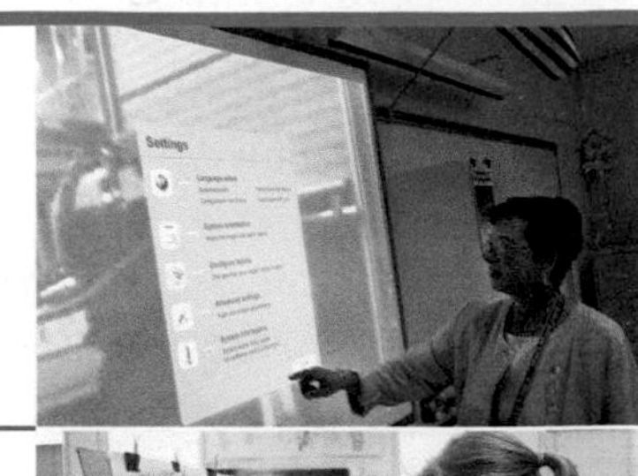

Synonyms

- combine; blend; unite; mix; incorporate

- During art, our teacher asked us to **integrate** shadows into our

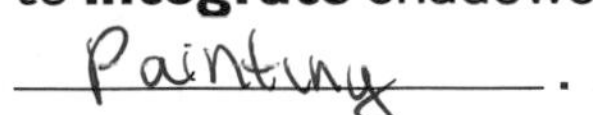

Painting.

Forms

- **Present:**
  - I/You/We/They integrate
  - He/She/It integrates
- **Past:** integrated

Family

- **Noun:** integration
- **Adjective:** integrated

Word Partners

- fully integrate
- integrate (someone/something) into

Examples

- The new video game **fully integrates** 3D special effects and graphics.
- When Loretto High School closed, Rio Americano High School immediately **integrated the students into** its classes.

Try It

My grandmother's doctor recommended that she **integrate** more green leaves ________ into her diet.

VERBAL PRACTICE

Talk about it **Discuss ideas with your partner, listen to classmates, and then write your favorite idea.**

Discuss
Listen
Write

1. It takes time ______________ to **integrate** new words into your vocabulary.

2. Our school should **integrate** more Sports ______________ classes into our academic program.

integrate

verb

WRITING PRACTICE

Collaborate

Discuss
Agree
Write
Listen

Discuss ideas with your partner and agree on the best words to complete the frame.

From our perspective, it would be beneficial to integrate news articles about real world into our English class.

Our Turn

Discuss
Listen
Write

Read the prompt. Work with the teacher to complete the frames. Write a thoughtful response that includes a convincing reason.

PROMPT: How would you help new students fully integrate into your school?

One way I would help new students fully integrate into our school would be by involving them in sports. In addition, I would suggest that they try to particpate in ~~sports~~ Team then call games with other students.

Be an Academic Author

Write
Discuss
Listen

Read the prompt and complete the frames. Strengthen your response with a convincing reason

PROMPT: Describe a time when you received a new article of clothing that meant a lot to you. How did you integrate it into an outfit that you wore to an important event?

Once, I received a new article of clothing Jean Jacket that meant a lot to me.
I integrated it into my outfit by wearing it with (a/an) white pant when I went to (a/an) a party. art show.

Construct a Response

Write
Discuss
Listen

Read the prompt and brainstorm ideas for a thoughtful response. Construct a response that includes relevant examples.

PROMPT: Computers enable people to make more effective presentations. What forms of media should students integrate into their presentations to engage and inform their audience?

To engage and inform their audience, students should integrate videos to make a more effective presentation. In this manner, they can ~~are able to~~ understand the subject.

grammar tip

Use the **modal verb**, or helping verb, *would* to show that something is possible under certain conditions. When you use *would*, add a verb in the base form.

EXAMPLE: If I won a new bike, I **would ride** it to school, then I **would show** it to my friends.

solve

verb

***Say it:* solve**

 ***Write it:*** ____________ ***Write it again:*** ____________

 ____________

TOOLKIT

Meaning

to find the correct answer to a question or problem

Examples

- My teacher asked me to ____________ how to **solve** the problem on the board.

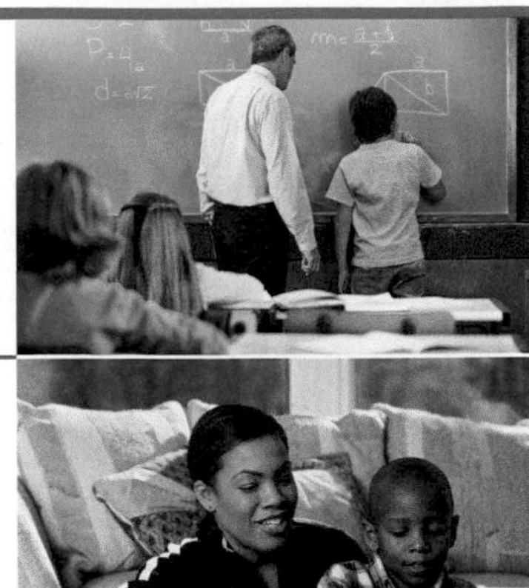

- The little boy tried to **solve** the puzzle by turning the pieces until they ____________.

Synonyms

- figure out

Forms

- **Present:**
  I/You/We/They solve
  He/She/It solves
- **Past:** solved

Family

- **Noun:** solution
- **Adjective:** solvable

Word Partners

- solve (a/the) problem
- try to solve

Examples

- The new pitcher may **solve the team's problem** by throwing a strike.
- I am **trying to solve** the equation in less than two minutes.

 **Try It**

During the science fair, many students tried to **solve** environmental problems by offering projects about ____________.

VERBAL PRACTICE

Talk about it — **Discuss ideas with your partner, listen to classmates, and then write your favorite idea.**

Discuss
Listen
Write

1. Detectives try to **solve** crimes using by investigating.
2. It is crucial that communities plan ahead to **solve** problems that might arise when a natural disaster, such as (a/an) Earthquake, strikes.

WRITING PRACTICE

Collaborate

Discuss
Agree
Write
Listen

Discuss ideas with your partner and agree on the best words to complete the frame.

One method that student pairs might use to solve a difficult problem is to analyze all the information.

Our Turn

Discuss
Listen
Write

Read the prompt. Work with the teacher to complete the frame. Write a thoughtful response that includes a relevant example.

PROMPT: Think about a favorite book or movie in which the characters had to solve a problem. What was the problem and how did they solve it?

In my favorite (book/movie) Titanic, the characters solved the problem of sinking the ship. They did this by using resources to save their lives.

Be an Academic Author

Write
Discuss
Listen

Read the prompt and complete the frames. Strengthen your response with relevant examples.

PROMPT: Think about how you would solve a problem that occurs between two friends at a party. Describe the problem, and explain two steps that would help you solve it.

From my perspective, if a problem occurred between two friends at a school Party party, I would want to Solve the problem. First, I would find a place where my friends could attend, and then I would ask them to have a conversation.

Construct a Response

Write
Discuss
Listen

Read the prompt and brainstorm ideas for a thoughtful response. Construct a response that includes relevant examples.

PROMPT: Tensions can arise among students working in groups, particularly when someone isn't contributing. What can the other group members do to effectively solve this common problem?

If someone isn't contributing to the science project, tensions can arise among students working in a group. The other group members can solve this problem by remainding them to respect the rules.

grammar tip

A common noun names a person, place, thing, or idea. **Singular nouns** name one person, place, thing, or idea. The words *a*, *an*, *the*, and *one* often appear before a singular noun.

EXAMPLE: The dog chased **the cat** until **an elderly neighbor** shouted, "STOP!"

strategy

noun

Say it: stra • te • gy

Write it: ______________________ **Write it again:** ______________________

 ______________________

TOOLKIT

Meaning

a plan to reach a goal

Examples

- The __________ team listened while their coach explained her new **strategy**.

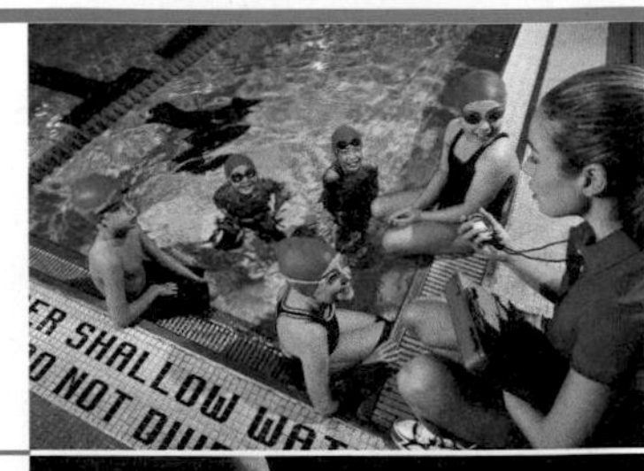

Synonyms

- plan; approach; design; method

- Watching her uncles helped Anika learn an effective **strategy** for winning at __________.

Forms

- **Singular:** strategy
- **Plural:** strategies
- **Verb:** strategize
- **Adjective:** strategic
- **Adverb:** strategically

Word Partners

- develop a strategy
- an effective strategy

Examples

- After the flood, the community **developed a strategy** for dealing with excessive rain.
- If you want to advertise a yard sale, **an effective strategy** is to put up posters around your neighborhood.

 **Try It**

As part of our social studies project on the invention of the Computer, we had to describe a possible **strategy** that the inventor could have used to test it.

VERBAL PRACTICE

Talk about it **Discuss ideas with your partner, listen to classmates, and then write your favorite idea.**

Discuss
Listen
Write

1. If you want the teacher to call on you, an effective **strategy** is to be ready for discussion time.

2. From my perspective, Soccer is a game that involves a lot of **strategy**.

strategy

noun

WRITING PRACTICE

Collaborate

Discuss
Agree
Write
Listen

Discuss ideas with your partner and agree on the best words to complete the frame.

The company developed several effective strategies to get people to not be involved in the Union.

Our Turn

Discuss
Listen
Write

Read the prompt. Work with the teacher to complete the frames. Write a thoughtful response that includes a personal experience.

PROMPT: Describe a time when you were unsure about how to solve a problem. What are two effectives strategies that you used to finally solve the problem?

Once, I was unsure about how to solve a/an difficult problem. So, two effective strategies I used to solve it were to ask (a/my) friend for help and to reread the direction.

Be an Academic Author

Write
Discuss
Listen

Read the prompt and complete the frames. Strengthen your response with a convincing reason.

PROMPT: Imagine that a friend arrived late to school several times because he/she overslept. What is an effective strategy you could suggest to your friend.

If a friend arrived late to school several times, one effective strategy I would suggest to help (him/her) wake up earlier would be to use a clock. In my opinion, this will only be an effective strategy if my friend listensed my advice.

Construct a Response

Write
Discuss
Listen

Read the prompt and brainstorm ideas for a thoughtful response. Construct a response that includes relevant examples.

PROMPT: Supermarkets have various strategies to encourage customers to spend more money. What are two effective strategies that target children shopping with their parents?

Supermarkets have various strategies to encourage customers to spend more money. In my opinion, Two effective strategies that target children shopping with their parents are free coupons and subtle advertising.

grammar tip

Adjectives are always singular even if they describe a plural noun. Do not add **-s** to adjectives that describe plural nouns.

EXAMPLE: My **tiny** kittens enjoy sleeping on **soft** blankets and eating **salmon** treats.

contribution

SMARTSTART

REVIEW: process *noun*

DAY 1

My first step in the ______________ of cleaning my room is to ______________________________.

contribution *noun*

DAY 2

If someone asked me to make a ______________ to the school bake sale, I'd probably prepare ______________________________.

DAY 3

Last year, our school held a ______________ drive to help needy families in our community, and many people in my neighborhood made significant ______________.

DAY 4

One person who made a major ______________ to science was ______________.

DAY 5

The ______________ team's performance was affected because some members were making far fewer ______________ than others.

TOTAL

SMART START

REVIEW: contribution *noun*

DAY 1

In order for an annual fundraiser to be successful, all of the participants need to work together and make equal contribution.

develop *verb*

DAY 2

My teacher asked me to develop my English essay by adding more details.

DAY 3

How long does it take for larvae to develop into adult trout?

DAY 4

I'm trying to develop my writing skills by practicing regularly and watching instructional videos.

DAY 5

If I could develop skills in any area, I would want to learn how to Write well.

TOTAL

select

SMART START

REVIEW: develop *verb*

DAY 1

You can develop muscle strength by

Work out every day.

select *verb*

DAY 2

When you select a restaurant for a special occasion, you should

consider the price and the menu.

DAY 3

My parents attended a raffle to raise money for

the church, and their ticket was randomly Selected

during the prize drawing.

DAY 4

During student council elections, many students Select the

candidates who have better plans.

DAY 5

I was very proud when my teacher selected my

Sciene project to show to the class as an example of a job well done.

TOTAL

SMARTSTART

REVIEW: select *verb*

DAY 1

When I select a snack from a vending machine, I usually look ☐

for something healthy. ☐

integrate *verb*

DAY 2

People who want to sleep better should integrate a relaxing ☐

activity such as soft music into their daily routine. ☐

DAY 3

In my opinion, a great song integrates powerful lyrics with ☐

sounds. ☐

DAY 4

When mixing the ingredients, you must make sure the

ingredients have been fully integrated or the final product may ☐

turn out poorly. ☐

DAY 5

One way to help integrate new neighbors into the neighborhood might ☐

be to invite to the weekly meeting. ☐

TOTAL

solve

SMART START

REVIEW: **integrate** *verb*

DAY 1

In my opinion, the best teachers are the ones who integrates some visitors into the lesson.

solve *verb*

DAY 2

By the end of a detective story, the main character has usually followed the clues and ________ the ________.

DAY 3

A good way to stimulate the brain is by trying to Solve a hard puzzle.

DAY 4

Once, I forgot about a project until the night before it was due, but I sowed the problem by ~~spending~~ working not sleeping and doing it.

DAY 5

A friend accidentally spilled soda on my shirt at lunch, but I solve the problem by washing.

TOTAL

SMART START

REVIEW: solve *verb*

DAY 1

Instead of calling an expert, my father tried to ___solve___ the problem with his ________ on his own and it took five hours to fix. ☐ ☐

strategy *noun*

DAY 2

One ___strategy___ you could use to make sure you leave on time for school in the morning would be to ___set the Alarm___ the night before. ☐ ☐

DAY 3

Several students may have different ___strategies___ for ___studying___, and they can all be equally successful. ☐ ☐

DAY 4

My brother became frustrated when his ___strategy___ for winning at ___the competition___ didn't work. ☐ ☐

DAY 5

The fascinating ___instinct___ has a unique ___strategy___ for capturing its prey. ☐ ☐

TOTAL

Toolkit Unit 6 | Compare and Contrast

Compare and Contrast

To ***compare*** two or more things, analyze what is the same.

To ***contrast*** two or more things, analyze what is different.

Find It **Compare** cats and dogs and circle what is the same.

Cats and Dogs

- are mammals
- can climb trees
- have four legs

Try It **Contrast** what is different about cats and dogs by adding ideas to each list.

Cats	Dogs
• are related to tigers	• are related to wolves
• are usually independent	• are usually social
• can help humans by ______________	• can help humans by ______________

RATE WORD KNOWLEDGE

Rate how well you know Toolkit words you'll use to compare and contrast.

RATE IT

6th Grade	BEFORE	7th Grade	AFTER	8th Grade
differ	1 2 3 4	**advantage**	1 2 3 4	aspect
equivalent	1 2 3 4	**compatible**	1 2 3 4	comparable
distinguish	1 2 3 4	**correspond**	1 2 3 4	draw
contrast	1 2 3 4	**distinguish**	1 2 3 4	distinction
share	1 2 3 4	**problematic**	1 2 3 4	comparison
distinct	1 2 3 4	**viewpoint**	1 2 3 4	direct

DISCUSSION GUIDE

- Form groups of four.
- Assign letters to each person.
- Each group member takes a turn leading a discussion.
- Prepare to report about one word.

A B D C

DISCUSS WORDS

Discuss how well you know the seventh grade words. Then, report to the class how you rated each word.

GROUP LEADER **Ask**

So, ________ (NAME) what do you know about the word ________ ?

GROUP MEMBERS **Discuss**

1 = I **don't recognize** the word ________ .
I need to learn what it means.

2 = I **recognize** the word ________ ,
but I need to learn the meaning.

3 = I'm **familiar** with the word ________ .
I think it means ________ .

4 = I **know** the word ________ .
It's a ________ (PART OF SPEECH), and it means ________ .
Here is my example sentence: ________ .

REPORTER **Report Word Knowledge**

Our group gave the word the competition a rating of ________ because ________ .

SET A GOAL AND REFLECT

First, set a vocabulary goal for this unit by selecting at least three words that you plan to thoroughly learn. At the end of the unit, return to this page and write a reflection about one word you have mastered.

GOAL

During this unit I plan to thoroughly learn the words ________ , ________ , and ________ . Increasing my word knowledge will help me speak and write effectively when I compare and difference.

REFLECTION

As a result of this unit, I feel most confident about the word ________ .

This is my model sentence: ________ .

advantage

noun

Say it: ad • **van** • tage

Write it: ______________ **Write it again:** ______________

 ______________

TOOLKIT

Meaning	**Examples**	
a positive quality or benefit	• Eagles have the **advantage** of ______________ eyesight, which helps them spot prey from far away.	
Synonyms • benefit **Antonyms** • disadvantage	• Mary uses her height to her **advantage** when ______________ with her synchronized swim team.	

Forms
- **Singular:** advantage
- **Plural:** advantages

Family
- **Adjective:** advantageous

Word Partners	**Examples**
• have an advantage over	• The U.S. Women's Gymnastics Team **has an advantage over** the other teams because they've been training for many years.
• use something to (my/your/his/her/our/their) advantage	• Emily studied Spanish during elementary school, and she **used it to her advantage** when studying Latin in middle school.

 **Try It**

Being tall is an **advantage** in a sport like ______________.

VERBAL PRACTICE

Talk about it — Discuss / Listen / Write

Discuss ideas with your partner, listen to classmates, and then write your favorite idea.

1. To prepare for the c best exam, our teacher encouraged us to use our notes and homework assignments to our **advantage**.
2. One **advantage** to waking up early is that you have more time to take breakfast.

advantage

noun

WRITING PRACTICE

Collaborate

Discuss
Agree
Write
Listen

Discuss ideas with your partner and agree on the best words to complete the frame.

My aunt used her knowledge of the geography to her advantage when planning a sightseeing trip for our family.

Our Turn

Discuss
Listen
Write

Read the prompt. Work with the teacher to complete the frames. Write a thoughtful response that includes convincing reasons.

PROMPT: Identify a popular and talented professional athlete that you admire. What are two advantages that this athlete seems to have when competing in his/her sport?

One popular and talented professional athlete that I admire is Michael Jordan ______. Two skills (he/she) she has over other athletes are the ability to collaborate with others and to ______ organize better than any other competitor.

Be an Academic Author

Write
Discuss
Listen

Read the prompt and complete the frames. Strengthen your response with a convincing reason.

PROMPT: Describe one advantage to living in a city. Identify a related feature, such as gorgeous parks or efficient public transportation, and explain how it enhances life in the city.

One advantage to living in a city is that you can find varied stores. In particular, being close to a city you can adore provides lots of opportunities to ______ ______.

Construct a Response

Write
Discuss
Listen

Read the prompt and brainstorm ideas for a thoughtful response. Include a personal experience to strengthen your response.

PROMPT: There are many advantages to having a smart phone. Describe the academic advantages of smart phones as a learning tool for teenagers taking challenging classes.

The academic advantages of smart phones as a learning tool for teenagers are students could use as a calculator,

grammar tip

The **preposition to** needs to be followed by a verb in the base form.

EXAMPLE: If you want **to explore** a museum, it's important **to read** the description near each exhibit.

compatible

adjective

Say it: com • **pat** • i • ble

Write it: ______________ ***Write it again:*** ______________

____

TOOLKIT

Meaning

when two things or people work well together

Examples

- Some animals are not **compatible**, but my dog and cat are great friends.

Antonyms

- incompatible

- The results of her science experiments are compatible with her classmates' results.

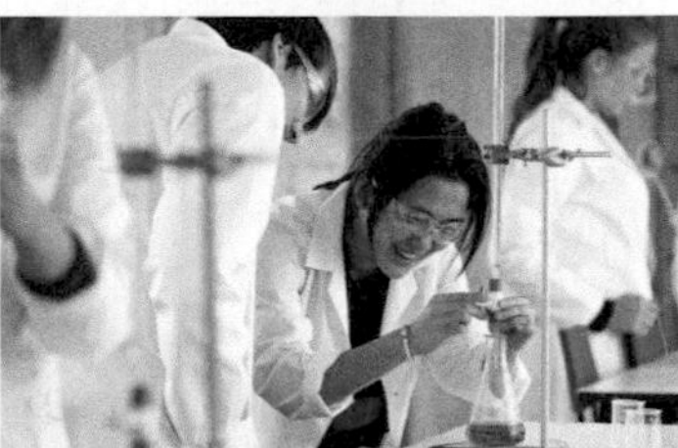

Family

- **Noun:** compatibility

Word Partners

- compatible with
- completely compatible

Examples

- The new game app is **compatible with** my cell phone.
- Our dreams are not always **completely compatible** with reality.

Try It

Outgoing people are usually most **compatible** with people who are opened - mind.

VERBAL PRACTICE

Talk about it **Discuss ideas with your partner, listen to classmates, and then write your favorite idea.**

Discuss
Listen
Write

1. When working in groups, it is productive to have classmates who have **compatible** ideas about science.

2. I have two friends who have completely **compatible** personalities because they both enjoy sharing ideas.

compatible

adjective

WRITING PRACTICE

Collaborate

Discuss
Agree
Write
Listen

Discuss ideas with your partner and agree on the best words to complete the frame.

When planning a meal, it is important to consider foods that have great tastes, such as lasagna and steak.

Our Turn

Discuss
Listen
Write

Read the prompt. Work with the teacher to complete the frames. Write a thoughtful response that includes a personal experience.

PROMPT: Describe a time in the past when something happened that made you realize that you might not be compatible with a friend. What did you do?

Some time ago, I realized that I might not be compatible with a friend when (he/she) She didn't share her ideas.

It was a tough experience, but I decided to be cautious with her..

Be an Academic Author

Write
Discuss
Listen

Read the prompt and complete the frames. Strengthen your response with a convincing reason.

PROMPT: Imagine you are planning the perfect outfit to wear to an important event. Describe two articles of clothing that are completely compatible when worn together.

When planning the perfect outfit to wear to (a/an) important event ________, I would include my favorite dress and my shoes. The reason these items are completely compatible is that they have similar color.

Construct a Response

Write
Discuss
Listen

Read the prompt and brainstorm ideas for a thoughtful response. Include relevant examples to strengthen your response.

PROMPT: Consumers should consider compatibility when selecting a new computer. What hardware and software do you own that must be compatible with your new computer's operating system?

When selecting a new computer, consumers should consider hardware and software that must be compatible with the computer's operating system.

grammar tip

The **preposition *to*** needs to be followed by a verb in the base form.

EXAMPLE: In my opinion, the best way **to cook** eggs is **to scramble** them with cheese.

correspond

verb

Say it: cor • re • **spond**

 ***Write it:*** ______________ ***Write it again:*** ______________

 ______________

TOOLKIT

Meaning

to agree or match

Examples

- The office of prime minister in Great Britain **corresponds** to ___be___ in the United States.

Synonyms

- match

- Many people are happy that the movie closely **corresponds** to the ___old version___.

Forms

- **Present:**
  I/You/We/They correspond
  He/She/It corresponds
- **Past:** corresponded

Family

- **Nouns:** correspondence
- **Adjective:** corresponding

Word Partners

- correspond to/with
- closely/directly correspond to

Examples

- The job of a goalie in water polo **corresponds to** a goalkeeper in soccer.
- The color of his cat **closely corresponds to** the color of my kitten.

 **Try It**

In the old grading system, a score of 85% **corresponded** to a B in our ___Saence___ class.

VERBAL PRACTICE

Talk about it **Discuss ideas with your partner, listen to classmates, and then write your favorite idea.**

Discuss
Listen
Write

1. I think the character of ___Harri's Poter___ in the movie closely **corresponds** to the same character in the book.

2. Getting to school on time usually **corresponds** to how quickly I'm able to ___wake early___.

correspond

verb

WRITING PRACTICE

Collaborate

Discuss
Agree
Write
Listen

Discuss ideas with your partner and agree on the best words to complete the frame.

Usually, a n imaginative / a caring personality correspond to a profession in art / teaching.

Our Turn

Discuss
Listen
Write

Read the prompt. Work with the teacher to complete the frames. Write a thoughtful response that includes a personal experience.

PROMPT: Describe what you do prior to taking a major test. How do these activities closely correspond to the grade you receive?

Prior to taking a major test, I review prior quizzes and practice answering questions by making flash cards.

These activities closely correspond to the grade I receive because when I feel thoroughly prepared, I usually earn a (good/bad) good grade.

Be an Academic Author

Write
Discuss
Listen

Read the prompt and complete the frames. Strengthen your response with a convincing reason.

PROMPT: Describe a movie or book character whose personality closely corresponds to yours.

From my perspective, the character Donkey in the (book/movie) book Shrek has a personality that closely corresponds to mine. One reason for this is that we both always try to look at the bright side.

Construct a Response

Write
Discuss
Listen

Read the prompt and brainstorm ideas for a thoughtful response. Include a personal experience to strengthen your response.

PROMPT: Avid fans of a book series want movie adaptations to closely correspond to the original story. Describe a movie that disappointed you because it significantly changed some details.

From my perspective, the movie "The life of Miguel" closely doesn't correspond to his life. That movie has changed some details.

grammar tip

An **adjective** describes, or tells about, a noun. An adjective sometimes appears after verbs such as *is, are, look, feel, smell,* and *taste.*

EXAMPLE: It is **impossible** not to gobble up freshly baked cookies as they smell **good** and taste **amazing**.

distinguish

verb

Say it: dis • **tin** • guish

Write it: ____________ ***Write it again:*** ____________

____

Meaning

to see or notice the difference between people or things

Synonyms

- recognize; understand

Examples

- You can **distinguish** between male and female lions by looking for the male's furry mane.

- Sometimes, it is difficult to **distinguish** between a turtle and a tortoise.

TOOLKIT

Forms

- **Present:**
  I/You/We/They distinguish
  He/She/It distinguishes
- **Past:** distinguished

Family

- **Adjective:** distinguishable, distinguished

Word Partners

- be difficult/easy to distinguish between
- have difficulty/trouble distinguish (something) from (something else)

Examples

- Some children think it is **difficult to distinguish between** right and left.
- Many people with vision disabilities **have trouble distinguishing red from green**.

Try It

It is easy to **distinguish** between snails and frogs because they have different colors and sizes.

VERBAL PRACTICE

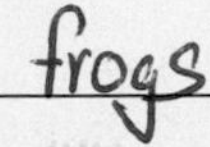

Talk about it **Discuss ideas with your partner, listen to classmates, and then write your favorite idea.**

Discuss
Listen
Write

1. Many people have difficulty **distinguishing** facts from opinions when reading social media comments about celebrities like Kim Kardshan.

2. One way to **distinguish** between hummingbirds and eagles is compare the size of their feathers.

distinguish

verb

WRITING PRACTICE

Collaborate

Discuss
Agree
Write
Listen

Discuss ideas with your partner and agree on the best words to complete the frame.

After the art show, our teacher tried diligently to distinguish between two drawing that did not include the names of the artists.

Our Turn

Discuss
Listen
Write

Read the prompt. Work with the teacher to complete the frames. Write a thoughtful response that includes relevant examples.

PROMPT: Think about the differences between a rainforest and a desert. Is it easy or difficult to distinguish between them? Describe a few features that distinguish one from the other.

It is relatively easy to distinguish between a rainforest and desert. For example, a rainforest landscape includes exotic plants, while an arid desert climate makes it challenging for plants and animals to thrive.

Be an Academic Author

Write
Discuss
Listen

Read the prompt and complete the frames. Strengthen your response with relevant examples.

PROMPT: Describe a favorite television show, or a board or video game, in which players compete against each other. What distinguishes your favorite from other shows or games?

One (show/game) game that I enjoy is monopoly. Two things that distinguish it from other (shows/games) games are that it is exciting, and it includes challenges when competitors try to buy more items.

Construct a Response

Write
Discuss
Listen

Read the prompt and brainstorm ideas for a thoughtful response. Include relevant examples to strengthen your response.

PROMPT: Successful entertainers and athletes have qualities that distinguish them. Select one celebrity you admire and describe what distinguishes this individual from his or her rivals.

One artist that I admire is: Sdine Dion. Two traits that distinguish her from other artists are that she posses an incridible voice and is a humble individual.

grammar tip

An **adverb** can describe, or tell about, a verb or an adjective. Adverbs usually go after a verb to describe how the action is done and come before an adjective to describe its quality.

EXAMPLE: My brother ordered a **really** big salad for lunch that he proceeded to eat **completely**.

problematic

adjective

Say it: prob • lem • **at** • ic

 **Write it:** ____________ **Write it again:** ____________

 ____________

TOOLKIT

Meaning

full of problems and difficult to deal with

Examples

- Air travel became **problematic** after the airport experienced a major power outage.

Synonyms

- difficult; tricky; troublesome

- After the snowstorm, drivers encountered a **problematic** situation on the steep, icy roads.

Family

- **Noun:** problem

Word Partners

- to be problematic
- a/the problematic situation

Examples

- It is clear that pest control in the apartment complex **is problematic** because we found ants crawling all over our food.
- Getting students back to school after the field trip became **a problematic situation** after the bus broke down.

 **Try It**

For younger learners, using the homophones there and they're correctly in a sentence can be **problematic.**

VERBAL PRACTICE

Talk about it **Discuss ideas with your partner, listen to classmates, and then write your favorite idea.**

Discuss Listen Write

1. A terrible storm would be **problematic** for young trick-or-treaters during Halloween.
2. If our school suddenly had fewer English teachers functioning computers, teaching would become a **problematic** situation.

problematic

adjective

WRITING PRACTICE

Collaborate

Discuss
Agree
Write
Listen

Discuss ideas with your partner and agree on the best words to complete the frame.

During the holidays, one problematic situation that people often experience is (a/an) crowded shopping mall/unexpected party invitation.

Our Turn

Discuss
Listen
Write

Read the prompt. Work with the teacher to complete the frames. Write a thoughtful response that includes a relevant example.

PROMPT: Think about one problematic situation that could occur on the job for a garbage collector. Describe it and suggest a solution.

One problematic situation that could occur on the job for a garbage collector is a mishap with (a/an) broken dompster lid. A solution I would suggest is to carefdly collecte the load.

Be an Academic Author

Write
Discuss
Listen

Read the prompt and complete the frames. Strengthen your response with a relevant example.

PROMPT: Describe what would happen if you just served your favorite dessert to a group of friends, and you realized that you forgot a crucial ingredient. Would it be problematic? What would you do?

If I just served my friends my favorite dessert, chocolate cate, and realized that I forgot to add ice cream it (would/would not) ________ be problematic. One reason is that the dessert would undoubtedly taste dried.

Construct a Response

Write
Discuss
Listen

Read the prompt and brainstorm ideas for a thoughtful response. Include a personal experience to strengthen your response.

PROMPT: Describe a time your family had to deal with a problematic situation while traveling. Explain how you overcame the problems.

While traveling to the beach, my family had to deal with a problematic situation to find a gasoline store. fourtanetely I had my bike on the car so I used it to get it.

grammar tip

A **common noun** names a person, place, thing, or idea. **Singular nouns** name one person, place, thing, or idea. The words *a, an, the,* and *one* often appear before a singular noun.

EXAMPLE: One school and **a grocery story** were closed today because of **the flood**.

viewpoint

noun

***Say it:* view • point**

Write it: ______________ ***Write it again:*** ______________

____

TOOLKIT

Meaning
the way someone thinks about something

Examples
- Most voters try to study the politicians' **viewpoints** before election day.

Synonyms
- view; opinion

- Students who enjoy expressing their particular **viewpoints** should consider joining the School club.

Forms
- **Singular:** viewpoint
- **Plural:** viewpoints

Word Partners
- express a viewpoint
- particular viewpoint

Examples
- The reporter **expressed a viewpoint** that surprised everyone.
- Most novels are told from one **particular viewpoint**.

Try It

I would enjoy reading a story told from the **viewpoints** of several different authors .

VERBAL PRACTICE

Talk about it — **Discuss ideas with your partner, listen to classmates, and then write your favorite idea.**

Discuss
Listen
Write

1. During Speech class, students are given time to express their **viewpoints**.

2. When conducting research for a report, it's important to study different **viewpoints** by reading valid facts.

viewpoint

noun

WRITING PRACTICE

Collaborate

Discuss
Agree
Write
Listen

Discuss ideas with your partner and agree on the best words to complete the frame.

After reading the book The prophecy, I hoped I could read a sequel that expressed the viewpoint of another character.

Our Turn

Discuss
Listen
Write

Read the prompt. Work with the teacher to complete the frames. Write a thoughtful response that includes a convincing reason.

PROMPT: Express your viewpoint about a school program that needs more funding. How would enhancing this program benefit students?

From the Viewpoint of a student attending this school, I would say that the school board needs to put more funding into the After school program.

Enhancing this program would benefit students by having more coach to help them read/ encouraging new ideas about coding.

Be an Academic Author

Write
Discuss
Listen

Read the prompt and complete the frames. Strengthen your response with a personal experience.

PROMPT: Describe a time when you heard someone express a viewpoint that was very different from your own. What happened next?

Once I heard someone express a very different viewpoint on the topic of saving water. As a result, I decided to share several facts so my classmates could consider my viewpoint.

Construct a Response

Write
Discuss
Listen

Read the prompt and brainstorm ideas for a thoughtful response. Include a personal experience to strengthen your response.

PROMPT: Many people regularly publish their opinions on the Internet. Describe the advantages of expressing your viewpoints on a social media blog rather than in a personal journal.

The advantages of expressing my ~~per~~ viewpoints on a social media blog rather than in a personal journal are that people could easily read it and also write back their comments.

grammar tip

A **past-tense verb** describes an action that already happened. For verbs that end in silent **e**, drop the final **e** before you add ***-ed***.

EXAMPLE: My cousin and I **disagreed** about the movie. I **loved** it, but she **hated** it.

advantage

SMART START

REVIEW: **strategy** *noun*

DAY 1

If you're lost in the woods, one strategy for finding your way back would be to use the GPS to guide you.

advantage *noun*

DAY 2

Famous celebrities face many challenges, but one advantage I think they have over ordinary people is that they can travel around the world..

DAY 3

I prefer training outdoors, but one advantage to having a gym membership is that you can meet people.

DAY 4

The winning team at the softball tournament had several scores over their opponents, including ______.

DAY 5

If you are stuck at home with a cold, you can use it to your advantage by catching up on your school homework.

TOTAL

compatible

SMART START

REVIEW: advantage *noun*

DAY 1

Being a diplomatic member is an advantage when traveling to another country.

compatible *adjective*

DAY 2

My old ~~brother~~ Computer is not compatible with the recent software upgrade.

DAY 3

My desire to go outside is not compatible with my need to stay inside and do my work. .

DAY 4

My brother and I have trouble agreeing on which movies or shows to watch because our tastes are not completely compatible.

DAY 5

Sheep and cows are two animals that are not Compatible.

TOTAL

correspond

SMARTSTART

REVIEW: compatible *adjective*

DAY 1

I'd like to learn how to excel in sports, which is completely compatible with my goal to exercise more often.

correspond *verb*

DAY 2

Your clothing should correspond to the occasion and the setting; for example, you shouldn't wear dress to your aunt's formal wedding.

DAY 3

A punishment should correspond to the offense; if a student is caught cheating on a test, he or she should suspend from the school.

DAY 4

What you eat often correspond directly to how you feel. If you eat a huge serving of bread, you're probably going to feel heavy or tired later.

DAY 5

People generally believe that the price of an item corresponds closely to its quality, but my parents bought an expensive bike that broke in less than a year.

TOTAL

distinguish

SMARTSTART

REVIEW: correspond *verb*

DAY 1

You could argue that the American peanut butter and jelly sandwich distinguish to the young individuals. ☐ ☐

distinguish *verb*

DAY 2

The forgery of the ________ was so convincing, even experts were not able to easily distinguish it from an original. ☐ ☐

DAY 3

The twins look identical, but one feature that makes it easy to distinguish between them is that one of them has curly hair. ☐ ☐

DAY 4

My sister and I share a room, but one thing that distinguishes my half of the room from hers is that it is organized. ☐ ☐

DAY 5

My teacher easily distinguishes me from my classmates. ☐ ☐

TOTAL

problematic

SMART START

REVIEW: **distinguish** *verb*

DAY 1

It can be difficult to distinguish between a chicken salad and a tuna salad sandwich unless you label them. ☐

problematic *adjective*

DAY 2

It would be quite problematic for a student to focus ☐

paid attention during class; our teacher would be furious. ☐

DAY 3

A problematic situation that you might encounter while biking in ☐

your town is (a/an) parade. ☐

DAY 4

Trying to organize a project / party can become

problematic when you have two close friends who don't get along ☐

with each other. ☐

DAY 5

What may seem like a minor illness can eventually become

problematic if you don't have it examined by a health care ☐

professional. ☐

TOTAL

SMART START

REVIEW: problematic *adjective*

DAY 1

It is a problematic situation to get on the school bus and realize that you have left your Snack on the kitchen counter. ☐ ☐

viewpoint *noun*

DAY 2

Your friends may have very different view point on important issues, but they should remember to express them in (a/an) explicit way. ☐ ☐

DAY 3

I would be in favor of a field trip to all students, but I'm not sure that many teachers or administrators would share my particular viewpoint. ☐ ☐

DAY 4

When I read a story told from someone else's ______, I can grow to understand and identify with someone completely different from me, such as (a/an) particular viewpoint. ☐ ☐

DAY 5

I do not share my parents' viewpoints that I should not be allowed to go out with my friends. ☐ ☐

TOTAL

Toolkit Unit 7 | Inference

Inference

To make an ***inference***, use a picture or information from the text and what we already know to form an idea.

Find It

Look at the picture above. Answer each question and make an inference.

What do you already know? +	What has happened in the picture? =	My inference
I already know that it can hurt when you fall off your bike.	The girl is ________ her leg and there is a bike in the background.	I think the girl has ________ off her bike.

Try It

Read the headline from the newspaper. Answer each question and make an inference.

Flu Shots Can Save Lives

What do you already know? +	What does the headline mean? =	My inference
I already know that the flu can be dangerous.	The headline means that people can decrease their risk of contracting the flu by getting a vaccine.	So this means I should make sure my family has (a/an) appointment to get flu shots.

RATE WORD KNOWLEDGE

Rate how well you know Toolkit words you'll use when you make inferences.

RATE IT

6th Grade	BEFORE	7th Grade	AFTER	8th Grade
determine	1 2 3 4	**conclusion**	1 2 3 4	expand
logical	1 2 3 4	**prediction**	1 2 3 4	perceive
generalize	1 2 3 4	**assumption**	1 2 3 4	generalization
involve	1 2 3 4	**infer**	1 2 3 4	perception
generalization	1 2 3 4	**imply**	1 2 3 4	presume
assume	1 2 3 4	**interpretation**	1 2 3 4	conclusion

DISCUSSION GUIDE

- Form groups of four.
- Assign letters to each person. A B D C
- Each group member takes a turn leading a discussion.
- Prepare to report about one word.

DISCUSS WORDS

Discuss how well you know the seventh grade words. Then, report to the class how you rated each word.

GROUP LEADER **Ask**

So, ______________ (NAME) what do you know about the word ______________ ?

GROUP MEMBERS **Discuss**

1 = I **don't recognize** the word ______________ .

I need to learn what it means.

2 = I **recognize** the word ______________ ,

but I need to learn the meaning.

3 = I'm **familiar** with the word ______________ .

I think it means ______________ .

4 = I **know** the word ______________ .

It's a ______________ (PART OF SPEECH) , and it means ______________ .

Here is my example sentence: ______________ .

REPORTER **Report Word Knowledge**

Our group gave the word ______________ a rating of ________ because ______________________ .

SET A GOAL AND REFLECT

First, set a vocabulary goal for this unit by selecting at least three words that you plan to thoroughly learn. At the end of the unit, return to this page and write a reflection about one word you have mastered.

GOAL

During this unit I plan to thoroughly learn the words ______________ , ______________ , and ______________ . Increasing my word knowledge will help me speak and write effectively when I make an ______________ .

REFLECTION

As a result of this unit, I feel most confident about the word ______________ .

This is my model sentence: ____ .

conclusion

noun

Say it: con • **clu** • sion

 ***Write it:*** ______________________ ***Write it again:*** ______________________

 ______________________

TOOLKIT

Meaning

a decision you make or an idea you have

Examples

- The teachers came to a **conclusion** about which field ______________ they would take next year.

- At the end of the trial, the ___team___ reached the **conclusion** that the defendant was not guilty.

Synonyms

- decision; judgment

Forms

- **Singular:** conclusion
- **Plural:** conclusions

Family

- **Verb:** conclude
- **Adjective:** concluding

Word Partners

- come to/reach the conclusion that
- draw a/the conclusion that

Examples

- The band **came to the conclusion that** they should do a carwash for their yearly fundraiser.
- When Samantha did not come to school for two days, we **drew the conclusion that** she was sick.

 **Try It**

After hearing the security guard ask visitors to step back from the ___stage___, we drew the **conclusion** that it was very fragile.

VERBAL PRACTICE

Talk about it

Discuss
Listen
Write

Discuss ideas with your partner, listen to classmates, and then write your favorite idea.

1. We thought making ___decoration___ for the party would be easy, but we soon came to the **conclusion** that they required a lot of skill.

2. After searching for my ___Science book___ for ten minutes, I reached the **conclusion** that I had left it at home.

conclusion

noun

WRITING PRACTICE

Collaborate
Discuss
Agree
Write
Listen

Discuss ideas with your partner and agree on the best words to complete the frame.

After reading different reviews about the upcoming movie, my mother came to the conclusion that it would be too scary for my little sister.

Our Turn
Discuss
Listen
Write

Read the prompt. Work with the teacher to complete the frames. Write a thoughtful response that includes a relevant example.

PROMPT: How would you help your family reach a conclusion about where to go for a vacation?

To plan a vacation, I would first ask my family members to name places to visit. For example, I would like to visit Italy. Then, we would vote to reach a Conclusion about where to go.

Be an Academic Author
Write
Discuss
Listen

Read the prompt and complete the frames. Strengthen your response with a personal experience.

PROMPT: Describe a time when you and a friend drew different conclusions about who should do something. What happened?

Once, a friend and I drew different conclosions about who should represent. It was awkward, but we decided to go together..

Construct a Response
Write
Discuss
Listen

Read the prompt and brainstorm ideas for a thoughtful response. Include a convincing reason to strengthen your response.

PROMPT: If every student in your math class performed poorly on a midterm exam, what conclusions would you draw?

If every student in my math class performed poorly on a midterm exam, I would draw the conclusion that they did not understand the lesson.

grammar tip

A **past tense verb** describes an action that already happened. Some verbs are irregular and change their spelling to form the past tense, such as *come* and *came*; *begin* and *began*; *draw* and *drew*.

EXAMPLE: I **came** home late after the soccer game and quickly **began** to do my homework.

prediction

noun

Say it: pre • **dic** • tion

Write it: ______________ ***Write it again:*** ______________

 ______________

TOOLKIT

Meaning

a statement about what you think will happen in the future

Examples

- During a presidential election, TV reporters often make **predictions** about who will win.

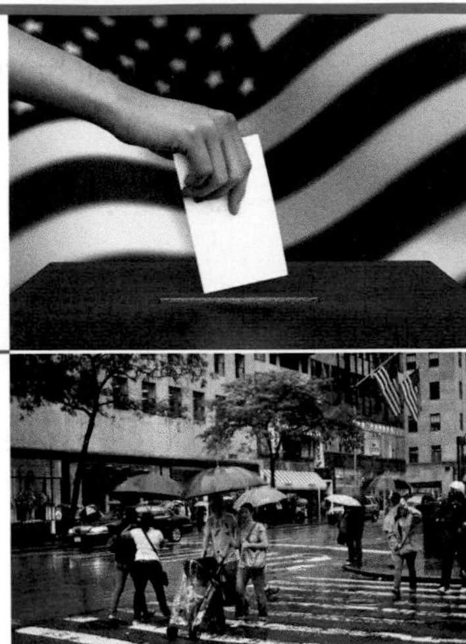

- The meteorologist made an accurate **prediction** about the weather today.

Synonyms

- guess

Forms

- **Singular:** prediction
- **Plural:** predictions

Family

- **Verb:** predict
- **Adjective:** predictable
- **Adverb:** predictably

Word Partners

- accurate prediction
- make a prediction

Examples

- The doctor made an **accurate prediction** about the baby's due date.
- Our teacher asked us to **make a prediction** about what would happen next in the story.

 **Try It**

When my father's cell phone screen cracked, he made an accurate **prediction** about how much it would cost to repair it.

VERBAL PRACTICE

Talk about it **Discuss ideas with your partner, listen to classmates, and then write your favorite idea.**

Discuss
Listen
Write

1. The latest **prediction** on social media is that Seline Dion will release a new song soon.

2. When I make **predictions** about the weather ______________, I am usually correct.

prediction

noun

WRITING PRACTICE

Collaborate
Discuss
Agree
Write
Listen

Discuss ideas with your partner and agree on the best words to complete the frame.

One prediction that we can confidently make about our class this month is that we will have to atend.

Our Turn
Discuss
Listen
Write

Read the prompt. Work with the teacher to complete the frames. Write a thoughtful response that includes a convincing reason.

PROMPT: Think about times when people have made predictions about the future of our planet. Did you listen? Why or why not?

When people have made predictions about the future of our planet, I (have/have not) listened their argument. One reason is that I think no one can predict it.

Be an Academic Author
Write
Discuss
Listen

Read the prompt and complete the frames. Strengthen your response with a convincing reason.

PROMPT: Make a prediction about something that you think will happen to you in the future. How do you know that you have made an accurate prediction?

One prediction I have about my future is that I will undoubtedly travel overseas. I'm confident that I've made an accurate prediction because I love to know dufferent places.

Construct a Response
Write
Discuss
Listen

Read the prompt and brainstorm ideas for a thoughtful response. Include a personal experience to strengthen your response.

PROMPT: An effective test-taking strategy is to predict key questions that will be included. What steps can you take in order to make accurate predictions about what to review for an upcoming test?

One step I can take in order to make accurate prediction ~~about~~ for an upcoming test is to ~~use~~ review old tests.

grammar tip

An **adverb** describes an action and can go before or after a verb. The adverbs *usually, often, shortly, confidently,* and *accurately* are examples of adverbs that can go before or after a verb.

EXAMPLE: My father **usually** cooks eggs for breakfast. He **often** scrambles them with chilies.

assumption

noun

Say it: as • **sump** • tion

 ***Write it:*** ______________ ***Write it again:*** ______________

 ______________

TOOLKIT

Meaning

an idea you have about something that is not always true

Synonyms

- conclusion

Examples

- After watching the Kittens playing, I made the **assumption** that they were from the same litter.

- A common **assumption** about boys is that they are less Shy, but that is inaccurate.

Forms

- **Singular:** assumption
- **Plural:** assumptions

Family

- **Verb:** assume
- **Adjective:** assumed

Word Partners

- make a/an false/accurate assumption
- common assumption

Examples

- Before they understood bacteria, doctors **made many false assumptions** about the causes of disease.
- A **common assumption** about sharks is that they like to eat humans, but scientists believe most attacks are accidental.

 **Try It**

I made an accurate **assumption** that the sport of ______________ is harder than it looks.

VERBAL PRACTICE

Talk about it **Discuss ideas with your partner, listen to classmates, and then write your favorite idea.**

Discuss
Listen
Write

1. A common **assumption** that people often make about animals like monkeys is that they are usually friendly.

2. If you see a long line at the Store, you can make an **assumption** that you will have to wait awhile.

assumption

noun

WRITING PRACTICE

Collaborate

Discuss
Agree
Write
Listen

Discuss ideas with your partner and agree on the best words to complete the frame.

When crossing the street, it is very dangerous to make an assumption that cars will always stop for you.

Our Turn

Discuss
Listen
Write

Read the prompt. Work with the teacher to complete the frames. Write a thoughtful response that includes a personal experience.

PROMPT: Describe an assumption that people often make about you that is inaccurate.

One inaccurate assumption that people often make about me is that I am not perseverant. Actually, I think I'm very perseverant because I enjoy doing my task.

Be an Academic Author

Write
Discuss
Listen

Read the prompt and complete the frames. Strengthen your response with a convincing reason.

PROMPT: Think about a famous person. What is a common assumption people make about this celebrity? Is this assumption accurate? Why or why not?

A common assumption people make about celebrities like Lucero ________ is that (he/she) ________ is very talented.

This seems to be (accurate/inaccurate) ________ because (he/she) ________ often perform very well.

Construct a Response

Write
Discuss
Listen

Read the prompt and brainstorm ideas for a thoughtful response. Include a personal experience to strengthen your response.

PROMPT: People often make false assumptions about certain dog breeds based on limited or inaccurate information. Identify a breed that is misunderstood and criticize the common assumption.

A common assumption people make about pitbulls dogs like pitboll is that it is very aggresive because it often bites or hurts strange people.

grammar tip

An **adjective** describes, or tells about, a noun. An adjective sometimes appears after verbs such as *is, are, look, feel, smell,* and *taste.*

EXAMPLE: Hot cocoa made with melted chocolate is **richer** and tastes **smoother** than a powdered mix.

infer

verb

Say it: in • **fer**

 ***Write it:*** ______________________ ***Write it again:*** ______________________

 ______________________

TOOLKIT

Meaning

to decide that something is probably true because of what you hear, see, or read

Synonyms

- figure out; decide

Examples

- When her brother was excited about his ______________ card, she **inferred** that he had done well.
- After seeing the dark clouds, we can reasonably **infer** that it is about to ______________.

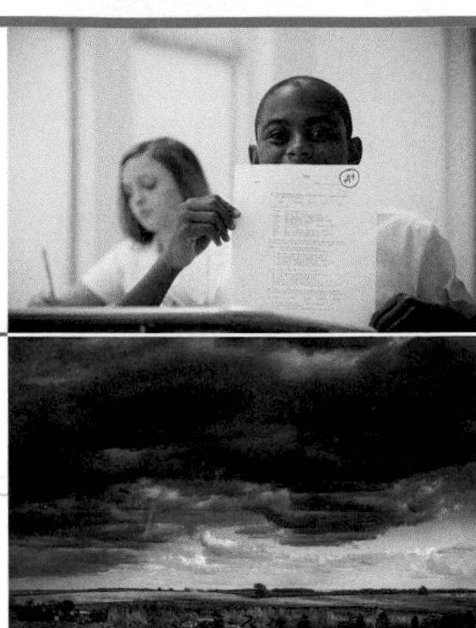

Forms

- **Present:**
  I/You/We/They infer
  He/She/It infers
- **Past:** inferred

Family

- **Noun:** inference

Word Partners

- can/could reasonably infer
- to infer from (something) that

Examples

- If you arrive to a restaurant and the lights are off, you **can reasonably infer** that it is closed.
- We **inferred from the arrival of a substitute that** our teacher was sick.

 **Try It**

When the basketball team came into the ice cream shop looking happy, we **inferred** that they had ____.

VERBAL PRACTICE

Talk about it **Discuss ideas with your partner, listen to classmates, and then write your favorite idea.**

Discuss
Listen
Write

1. My dad can usually **infer** when people aren't telling the truth by the way in which they ____.

2. When the principal calls a student to the office, the class can reasonably **infer** that the person is about to ____.

WRITING PRACTICE

Collaborate

Discuss
Agree
Write
Listen

Discuss ideas with your partner and agree on the best words to complete the frame.

To ____________________ the meaning of an unknown word, it's helpful to ____.

Our Turn

Discuss
Listen
Write

Read the prompt. Work with the teacher to complete the frames. Write a thoughtful response that includes a personal experience.

PROMPT: Describe a time in which you were able to infer how your friend was feeling based upon the look on his or her face.

Once I was able to ____________ from the look on my friend's face that (he/she) ________ was feeling quite ______________________________. After I offered a few words of ______________________________, my friend shared news about the ____.

Be an Academic Author

Write
Discuss
Listen

Read the prompt and complete the frames. Strengthen your response with relevant examples.

PROMPT: Imagine that you are an archaeologist digging up objects made by people in the past. What might you reasonably infer about the people?

If I were an archaeologist digging up objects such as ____________________ and ____________________________ made by people in the past, I might reasonably ____________ that they had (a/an) ____ ______________________ culture. For example, they might have enjoyed ____.

Construct a Response

Write
Discuss
Listen

Read the prompt and brainstorm ideas for a thoughtful response. Include a personal experience to strengthen your response.

PROMPT: Parents or caregivers can often infer what kind of day their child has had. What evidence could your family use to infer something about your school day?

____

____

____

grammar tip

The **preposition *to*** needs to be followed by a verb in the base form.

EXAMPLE: It is important **to eat** a healthy breakfast if you plan **to compete** in a soccer game.

imply

verb

Say it: im • **ply**

 ***Write it:*** ______________ ***Write it again:*** ______________

 ______________

TOOLKIT

Meaning

to suggest that something is true, without saying or showing it directly

Synonyms

- to suggest; to hint at

Examples

- The commercial **implies** that the Olympic gold medalist owes some of her success to her ______________.
- The judge's rigid body language seems to **imply** that she did not believe the ______________.

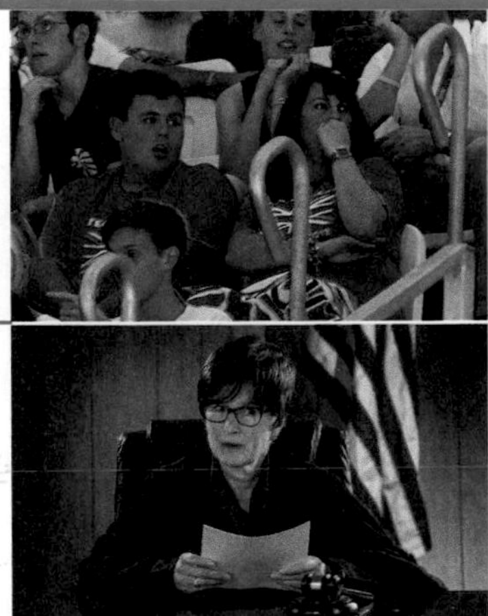

Forms

- **Present:**

I/You/We/They	imply
He/She/It	implies

- **Past:** implied

Family

- **Noun:** implication
- **Adjective:** implied

Word Partners

- seem to imply
- mean to/clearly imply

Examples

- His chest pain **seemed to imply** that he was having a heart attack.
- When you gave me soap for a present, did you **mean to imply** that I needed a bath?

 **Try It**

When a teacher recommends that the class should spend more time on homework, he might be **implying** that the ______________.

VERBAL PRACTICE

Talk about it Discuss ideas with your partner, listen to classmates, and then write your favorite idea.

Discuss
Listen
Write

1. When my friend commented that my ______________ looks "so much better now," she seemed to **imply** that it didn't look good before.

2. The TV ad for the new ______________ clearly **implies** that they are nutritious, but the labels indicate otherwise.

imply

verb

WRITING PRACTICE

Collaborate
Discuss
Agree
Write
Listen

Discuss ideas with your partner and agree on the best words to complete the frame.

Through the use of unusual statistics, the politician seems to ________________ that the nation's ________________ is in trouble, when actually it is quite good.

Our Turn
Discuss
Listen
Write

Read the prompt. Work with the teacher to complete the frames. Write a thoughtful response that includes a personal experience.
PROMPT: Describe a time when you made a suggestion that a friend should get something new, and you realized that you might have implied something negative.

Once, when I suggested that my friend should get some new ________________ ,

I didn't mean to ____________ that (he/she) ________ was ________________ .

Instead, I simply wanted my friend to ________________________ .

Be an Academic Author
Write
Discuss
Listen

Read the prompt and complete the frames. Strengthen your response with a personal experience.
PROMPT: Describe a time when you tried to help a younger relative or friend adjust his or her behavior using a nonverbal signal. What did you mean to imply?

Once I tried to help my younger ____________ adjust (his/her) ________ behavior by

____ . I meant to

____________ that (he/she) ________ should ________________________

and fortunately, (he/she) ________ got the message!

Construct a Response
Write
Discuss
Listen

Read the prompt and brainstorm ideas for a thoughtful response. Include relevant examples to strengthen your response.
PROMPT: Think about how body language can communicate something. What does a classmate's body language seem to imply when he rolls his eyes or raises his eyebrows during a lesson?

____

____

____

grammar tip

A **possessive noun** shows ownership. Possessive nouns always have apostrophes. For one owner, add **-'s** to a singular noun. For more than one owner, add an apostrophe (') to the end of the plural noun.

EXAMPLE: Many **girls'** birthday parties can be loud, but my little **sister's** party was very quiet.

interpretation

noun

Say it: in • ter • pre • **ta** • tion

 ***Write it:*** ______________________ ***Write it again:*** ______________________

 ______________________

TOOLKIT

Meaning

an explanation or opinion about what something means

Examples

- My friend and I had very __________ **interpretations** of the movie.

Synonyms

- understanding

- We reviewed each of our __________ to make sure we made an accurate **interpretation** of the data.

Forms

- **Singular:** interpretation
- **Plural:** interpretations

Family

- **Verb:** interpret
- **Adjective:** interpretable

Word Partners

- a correct/an accurate interpretation of
- interpretation of something

Examples

- Her graph was so precise that it was easy to make **an accurate interpretation of** the data.
- I trust my doctor's **interpretation of the results** of the blood test.

 **Try It**

Although we both read the same book, we seem to have different **interpretations** about the ______________________.

VERBAL PRACTICE

Talk about it — **Discuss ideas with your partner, listen to classmates, and then write your favorite idea.**

Discuss
Listen
Write

1. The referee had a very different **interpretation** of the ______________________ than the ______________________ team's coach.

2. If the baby girl is crying, it may be an accurate **interpretation** that she is ______________________.

interpretation

noun

WRITING PRACTICE

Collaborate

Discuss
Agree
Write
Listen

Discuss ideas with your partner and agree on the best words to complete the frame.

There are a wide variety of possible ______________ of the results of the ______________.

Our Turn

Discuss
Listen
Write

Read the prompt. Work with the teacher to complete the frames. Write a thoughtful response that includes a personal experience.

PROMPT: Describe a recent dream and your interpretation of what it means.

Recently, I had a dream about being able to ______________.

My ______________ of the dream is that it was encouraging me to ______________.

Be an Academic Author

Write
Discuss
Listen

Read the prompt and complete the frames. Strengthen your response with a relevant example.

PROMPT: Imagine a scenario in which a language learner makes an inaccurate interpretation of something she hears. Describe how she might react when she realizes her mistake.

I'm imagining a scenario in which a language learner makes an inaccurate ______________ of (a/an) ______ ______________. As she begins to reply, she can tell from the ______________ look on her listener's face that she should ______________.

Construct a Response

Write
Discuss
Listen

Read the prompt and brainstorm ideas for a thoughtful response. Include a personal experience to strengthen your response.

PROMPT: Principals and students frequently view dress code policies differently. Identify one fashion trend at your school that is open to a variety of interpretations by adults and teenagers.

____

____

____

grammar tip

Count nouns name things that can be counted. Count nouns have two forms, singular and plural. To make most count nouns plural, add **-s**. To make count nouns that end in *x, ch, sh, ss,* and *z* plural, add ***-es***.

EXAMPLE: My friend and I wore the same **pants** and **sweaters** to the **movies**.

conclusion

SMART START

REVIEW: viewpoint *noun*

DAY 1

Readers can share their ______________________ about an online article in the comments section, but many people express themselves in a very ______________________ way.

conclusion *noun*

DAY 2

My friend and I came to completely different ______________________ about the meaning of a character's ______________________ in the recent episode of our favorite TV show.

DAY 3

After listening to each side's arguments, our debate coach reached the ______________________ that ______________________ ______________________.

DAY 4

If a lot of students went home sick on the same day, one ______________________ I might draw is that ______________________ ______________________.

DAY 5

In science class the other day, we experimented with ______________________ ______________________, and then wrote all of our ______________________ in a report.

TOTAL

REVIEW: conclusion *noun*

DAY 1

When the food at the party disappeared within ten minutes, I reached the

____________________ that ____________________________

____________________.

prediction *noun*

DAY 2

When I accidentally broke a plate, I made an accurate ____________________

that my mother would ____.

DAY 3

One ____________________ I might make about this school year is that I will

____.

DAY 4

When watching (a/an) __________ ____________________ on TV, I like

to guess what will happen and then see if my ____________________ were

correct.

DAY 5

When our area receives a lot of rain, one ____________________ we can make

is that there will be ____.

TOTAL

assumption

SMART START

REVIEW: prediction *noun*

DAY 1

Before the ______________________________, my friends and I all made ______________________________ about which team would win.

assumption *noun*

DAY 2

One common ______________________________ many adults make about teenagers is that we aren't ______________________________.

DAY 3

It's not fair to make too many ______________________________ about people you don't know based on their ______________________________.

DAY 4

When I wasn't invited to my friend's ______________________________, I made the ______________________________ that she didn't want me there, when in reality the invitation had been sent to the wrong email.

DAY 5

If you come face to face with (a/an) __________ ______________________________ in your neighborhood, never make the ______________________________ that it is safe to approach.

TOTAL

SMARTSTART

REVIEW: assumption *noun*

DAY 1

Instead of making numerous ______________________ about people from another culture based on stereotypes, we should try to ______________________
______________________.

☐ ☐

infer *verb*

DAY 2

I ______________________ that my classmates were bored by the presentation because many of them were ______________________
______________________.

☐ ☐

DAY 3

When my brother walked in the door looking ______________________,
I correctly ______________________ that he had just been running.

☐ ☐

DAY 4

You can reasonably ______________________ how a dog is feeling by watching its ______________________.

☐ ☐

DAY 5

When you see a group of teens looking down at their cell phones, you could reasonably ______________________ that they are all ______________________
______________________.

☐ ☐

TOTAL

imply

SMART START

REVIEW: infer *verb*

DAY 1

If people kept staring at my hair, I would probably ________________ that ________________________________.

imply *verb*

DAY 2

The look on my father's face when he tasted the scrambled eggs seemed to ________________ that he didn't expect them to be so ________________.

DAY 3

I haven't read the feedback on my report yet, but all of the red ink on the page would seem to ________________ that ________________________________.

DAY 4

My friend's use of capital letters and exclamation points in her text message strongly ________________ that something ________________ was happening.

DAY 5

By repeatedly saying she cared about ________________________________, the presidential candidate meant to ________________ that her opponent did not share her views.

TOTAL

SMART START

REVIEW: imply *verb*

DAY 1

My friend complained about how long she waited for me, but the ______________________ on her face ______________________ that she wasn't really upset.

interpretation *noun*

DAY 2

My ______________________ of my mother's silence during the car ride was that she was feeling ______________________ .

DAY 3

Sometimes, various news outlets have different ______________________ of what happened during (a/an) __________ ______________________ ______________________ .

DAY 4

If you don't use ______________________ in your text messages, the other person's ______________________ of your language or tone could be completely inaccurate.

DAY 5

It's better to see your doctor if you are experiencing ______________________ ; medical websites may not provide an accurate ______________________ of your symptoms and cause you more anxiety.

TOTAL

Toolkit Unit 8 | Argument

Argument

To make an ***argument*** means to explain why you believe something is true by supporting it with convincing reasons, relevant examples, and personal experiences.

Find It **Read the sentences. Underline the best reason, example, or experience to support each argument.**

1. School sports teams should be co-ed.

a. Multiple studies show that participating in co-ed sports encourages mutual respect and understanding between genders.

b. Co-ed sports teams would allow schools with smaller student populations to compete in more sports.

c. Having boys and girls play sports together prevents gender stereotyping.

2. The majority of climate change is man-made.

a. People burn large amounts of fossil fuel for energy production and transportation.

b. If people decreased their energy consumption, we could reduce the amount of carbon dioxide in the atmosphere.

c. According to the science journal *Nature*, research shows that 74% of the increase in global temperatures is due to human activity.

Try It **Write one convincing reason to support the argument.**

People should not use electronic devices before going to sleep. One important reason is that using electronic devices before bed can ______________________________

______________________________.

RATE WORD KNOWLEDGE

Rate how well you know Toolkit words you'll use when you prepare to argue.

RATE IT

6th Grade	BEFORE	7th Grade	AFTER	8th Grade
claim	1 2 3 4	**point**	1 2 3 4	crucial
proof	1 2 3 4	**emphasis**	1 2 3 4	maintain
state	1 2 3 4	**justify**	1 2 3 4	opposition
emphasize	1 2 3 4	**logical**	1 2 3 4	principle
support	1 2 3 4	**relevance**	1 2 3 4	resolve
compelling	1 2 3 4	**valid**	1 2 3 4	sufficient

DISCUSSION GUIDE

- Form groups of four. Ⓐ Ⓑ
- Assign letters to each person. Ⓓ Ⓒ
- Each group member takes a turn leading a discussion.
- Prepare to report about one word.

DISCUSS WORDS

Discuss how well you know the seventh grade words. Then, report to the class how you rated each word.

GROUP LEADER Ask

So, ________ (NAME) what do you know about the word ________ ?

GROUP MEMBERS Discuss

1 = I **don't recognize** the word ________ .
I need to learn what it means.

2 = I **recognize** the word ________ ,
but I need to learn the meaning.

3 = I'm **familiar** with the word ________ .
I think it means ________ .

4 = I **know** the word ________ .
It's a ________ (PART OF SPEECH) , and it means ________ .
Here is my example sentence: ________ .

REPORTER Report Word Knowledge

Our group gave the word ________ a rating of ________ because ________ .

SET A GOAL AND REFLECT

First, set a vocabulary goal for this unit by selecting at least three words that you plan to thoroughly learn. At the end of the unit, return to this page and write a reflection about one word you have mastered.

GOAL

During this unit I plan to thoroughly learn the words ________ , ________ , and ________ . Increasing my word knowledge will help me speak and write effectively when I need to argue a point.

REFLECTION

As a result of this unit, I feel most confident about the word ________ .
This is my model sentence: ________
________ .

point

noun

Say it: point

Write it: ______________________ **Write it again:** ______________________

____

TOOLKIT

Meaning

a single idea, fact, or opinion that is part of an argument or decision

Synonyms

- idea; opinion

Examples

- Although I don't enjoy eating fruit, the doctor's **points** about the various ______________ benefits were compelling.

- A The recruiter made some interesting **points** about his university's ______________ program.

Forms

- **Singular:** point
- **Plural:** points

Word Partners

- make an/some interesting/ valid point that
- to make a good point

Examples

- During the debate, Miguel **made a valid point that** won the argument.
- My sister was able **to make a good point** about owning a computer that convinced my mom to buy one for our family.

Try It

The science fair judge complimented me for making some interesting **points** in my hypothesis, but she encouraged me to ______________________________ on my project board.

VERBAL PRACTICE

Talk about it **Discuss ideas with your partner, listen to classmates, and then write your favorite idea.**

Discuss
Listen
Write

1. We tried to make a good **point** about postponing the science exam, such as the high number of ______________________________ ______________________________, but our teacher disagreed.

2. One interesting **point** about video games is that they are ______________________________ ______________________________ to most teens.

WRITING PRACTICE

Collaborate

Discuss
Agree
Write
Listen

Discuss ideas with your partner and agree on the best words to complete the frame.

Last year, our teacher made a good ____________ about the importance of ____________
____.

Our Turn

Discuss
Listen
Write

Read the prompt. Work with the teacher to complete the frames. Write a thoughtful response that includes a personal experience.

PROMPT: Think about a time when you wanted to overcome a fear of something. When you talked to someone about your fear, what point did he or she offer to help you overcome it?

When I wanted to overcome my fear of ______________________________

______________, I talked to my ______________________ about it. One

interesting __________ (he/she) __________ offered to help me overcome my fear was to

____.

Be an Academic Author

Write
Discuss
Listen

Read the prompt and complete the frames. Strengthen your response with a relevant example.

PROMPT: Imagine that you desperately want a new, exotic pet. What is one good point that you can make to convince a parent or caregiver that you will be a responsible pet owner?

If I wanted a new, exotic pet, such as (a/an) ______________________, I would try to convince

my ____________ that I will be a responsible pet owner. One good __________ I can make is that

I can ____.

Construct a Response

Write
Discuss
Listen

Read the prompt and brainstorm ideas for a thoughtful response. Include relevant examples to strengthen your response.

PROMPT: Many legislators want to raise the driving age to 18 because of the number of fatalities involving reckless teen drivers. What points could you make against this argument?

____

____

____

grammar tip

Use a **verb + ing** after the prepositions *by*, *of*, and *for*.

EXAMPLE: The video showed different techniques **for tying** knots.

emphasis

noun

Say it: **em** • pha • sis

 ***Write it:*** ______________________ ***Write it again:*** ______________________

 ______________________

TOOLKIT

Meaning

the special importance given to something

Examples

- Our science teacher puts a lot of **emphasis** on ____________ whenever we work with chemicals.

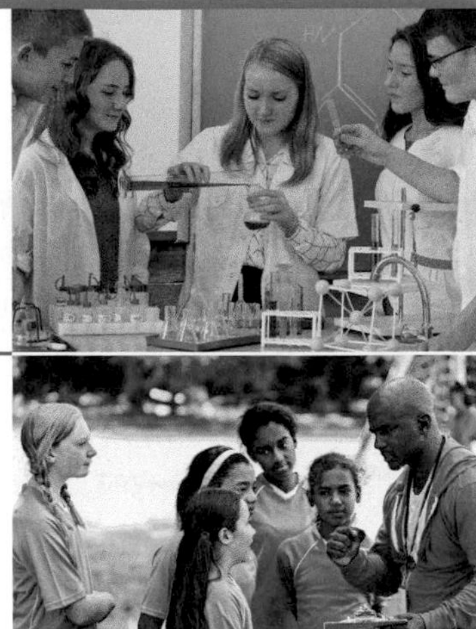

Synonyms

- significance

- Our coach places greater **emphasis** on teamwork than developing one star player.

Forms

- **Singular:** emphasis
- **Plural:** emphases

Family

- **Verb:** emphasize
- **Adjective:** emphatic

Word Partners

- place emphasis on
- put an emphasis on

Examples

- Our school **places emphasis on** students becoming global citizens.
- My parents **put an emphasis on** schoolwork over everything else.

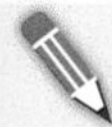 **Try It**

Of all my hobbies, I put the most **emphasis** on ______________________________.

VERBAL PRACTICE

Talk about it **Discuss ideas with your partner, listen to classmates, and then write your favorite idea.**

Discuss
Listen
Write

1. In many English classes, teachers usually place **emphasis** on reading ____________ ____________ and writing ______________________.

2. When my neighbor asked me to care for his ____________________, he placed **emphasis** on watering since the weather was expected to be over 100 degrees while he was away.

emphasis

noun

WRITING PRACTICE

Collaborate

Discuss
Agree
Write
Listen

Discuss ideas with your partner and agree on the best words to complete the frame.

Our school should pay less attention to playing sports and put greater ____________ on ____.

Our Turn

Discuss
Listen
Write

Read the prompt. Work with the teacher to complete the frames. Write a thoughtful response that includes a convincing reason.

PROMPT: Think about another subject, such as history or science. Describe an assignment that your teacher has placed an emphasis on. Why do you think this assignment is so important?

One assignment that our ____________________ teacher has placed an ____________ on is to ____ ____________________. The reason this is so important is because ____.

Be an Academic Author

Write
Discuss
Listen

Read the prompt and complete the frames. Strengthen your response with a relevant example.

PROMPT: Imagine that you are creating a travel brochure to promote your community. What two landmarks would you put emphasis on?

Two landmarks I would put ____________ on in a brochure to promote my community are the ______________________________ and the ______________ ______________. For example, I would take photographs of both locations and write (a/an) ______ ______________________________.

Construct a Response

Write
Discuss
Listen

Read the prompt and brainstorm ideas for a thoughtful response. Include relevant examples to strengthen your response.

PROMPT: It can be difficult to balance your school life and your personal life. What are the consequences of consistently placing greater emphasis on one part of your life over the other?

____

____

____

grammar tip

The **preposition *on*** links a noun, noun phrase, or pronoun to the other parts of a sentence.

EXAMPLE: I want to join a volleyball team this summer, but my parents think I should focus **on** finding a part-time job.

justify

verb

***Say it:* jus • ti • fy**

 ***Write it:*** ______________ ***Write it again:*** ______________

 ______________

TOOLKIT

Meaning

to give reasons why something is right or necessary

Examples

- Many adults **justify** spending money on coffee because they think it helps them wake up.

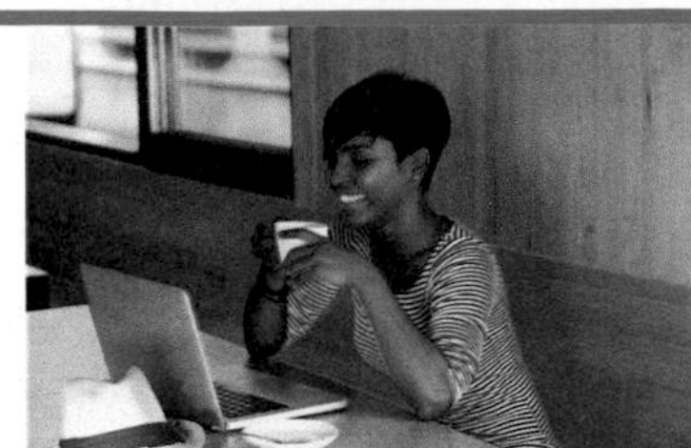

- My sister **justified** her need for a new backpack by showing our mom how her old one was a hole.

Forms

- **Present:**

I/You/We/They	justify
He/She/It	justifies

- **Past:** justified

Family

- **Noun:** justification
- **Adjective:** justifiable
- **Adverb:** justifiably

Word Partners

- justify why
- try/need/be difficult to justify

Examples

- If you arrive after the bell rings, you will be asked to **justify why** you are late.
- José found it **difficult to justify** how he lost the car keys.

 **Try It**

The principal **justified** why she expelled the student who was responsible for the recent violence at school.

VERBAL PRACTICE

Talk about it **Discuss ideas with your partner, listen to classmates, and then write your favorite idea.**

Discuss
Listen
Write

1. Sometimes people try to **justify** spending $50 each month on (a/an) high calories beverage because they think it helps them be more productive.
2. In most classes, you need to **justify** any missed appointment.

justify

verb

WRITING PRACTICE

Collaborate

Discuss
Agree
Write
Listen

Discuss ideas with your partner and agree on the best words to complete the frame.

Yesterday, we ______________ missing the field trip bus by explaining that we were

____.

Our Turn

Discuss
Listen
Write

Read the prompt. Work with the teacher to complete the frames. Write a thoughtful response that includes a personal experience.

PROMPT: Describe a recent time when you tried to justify why you forgot something but your friend, teacher, or parent did not believe you. What did you do?

Recently, I tried to ______________ why I forgot to ______________________________

______________________, but my ______________ did not believe me. So I apologized

and promised to ____.

Be an Academic Author

Write
Discuss
Listen

Read the prompt and complete the frames. Strengthen your response with a convincing reason.

PROMPT: Think of a book or movie character that you find intriguing, but who other people may not know about or find very interesting. Describe how you would justify your perspective.

One character I find intriguing is ______________________________ from

______________________________. One way to ______________ my perspective

is to explain how (he/she) __________ overcomes challenges by ______________

____.

Construct a Response

Write
Discuss
Listen

Read the prompt and brainstorm ideas for a thoughtful response. Include a convincing reason to strengthen your response.

PROMPT: Teenagers often lose or ruin their cell phones. How can you justify having your parents purchase a new, expensive cell phone for you after you lost or ruined your old one?

____

____

____

grammar tip

An **adjective** describes, or tells about, a noun. An adjective sometimes appears after verbs such as *is*, *are*, *look*, *feel*, *smell*, and *taste*.

EXAMPLE: My mother is **talented** as a gardener. Her vegetables always look **perfect**.

logical

adjective

Say it: **log • i • cal**

 ***Write it:*** ______________________ ***Write it again:*** ______________________

 ______________________

TOOLKIT

Meaning
using careful reasoning or good sense

Examples
- Adopting a __________ isn't a **logical** choice if you are allergic to them.

- There is no **logical** reason why our school cafeteria shouldn't offer ______________.

Synonyms
- rational; sensible

Antonyms
- illogical

Family
- **Noun:** logic
- **Adverb:** logically

Word Partners
- logical choice
- logical explanation/reason

Examples
- Since Veronica was the vice president of the glee club last year, selecting her for president this year was a **logical choice**.
- Two **logical reasons** for recycling are that it reduces garbage and allows us to reuse materials.

 **Try It**

One **logical** reason parents require their children to do chores is because ____.

VERBAL PRACTICE

Talk about it **Discuss ideas with your partner, listen to classmates, and then write your favorite idea.**

Discuss
Listen
Write

1. If you lose your ______________________, it is **logical** to retrace your steps until you find it.

2. Students must provide a **logical** explanation when returning to school after an absence, such as (a/an) __________ ______________________.

logical

adjective

WRITING PRACTICE

Collaborate

Discuss
Agree
Write
Listen

Discuss ideas with your partner and agree on the best words to complete the frame.

After discovering that my ______________________ wasn't in my backpack, one ______________ explanation could be that I left it at home.

Our Turn

Discuss
Listen
Write

Read the prompt. Work with the teacher to complete the frames. Write a thoughtful response that includes a convincing reason.

PROMPT: Some people claim to have seen UFOs. Provide a logical explanation for what they could have actually seen. Explain why they might have been confused.

When people claim to have seen UFOs, a ______________ explanation could be that they actually saw (a/an) __________ ______________________________. One reason for their confusion might be that they have ______________________ imaginations.

Be an Academic Author

Write
Discuss
Listen

Read the prompt and complete the frames. Strengthen your response with a relevant example.

PROMPT: Many parents and teens believe that classes start too early in the morning. Offer a logical argument for starting school at 9:00 am.

One ______________ argument for starting school at 9:00 am is that teens need to ____. With this change, most students could ______________________________ before school.

Construct a Response

Write
Discuss
Listen

Read the prompt and brainstorm ideas for a thoughtful response. Include two convincing reasons to strengthen your response.

PROMPT: Many high schools are requiring off-campus internships to explore career pathways. Identify an ideal setting for your internship and provide two logical reasons for your choice.

____

____

____

grammar tip

Use the **modal verb,** or helping verb, *could* to show that something might be possible. When you use *could*, add a verb in the base form.

EXAMPLE: My sister **could** eat nachos everyday. However, she **could** also gain weight.

relevance

noun

Say it: **rel** • e • vance

 ***Write it:*** ____________ ***Write it again:*** ____________

 ____________

TOOLKIT

Meaning
being directly related to a situation or topic

Examples
- Math actually has a lot of **relevance** in our everyday ________ .

- Mosquitos have a particular **relevance** for people living in ________ .

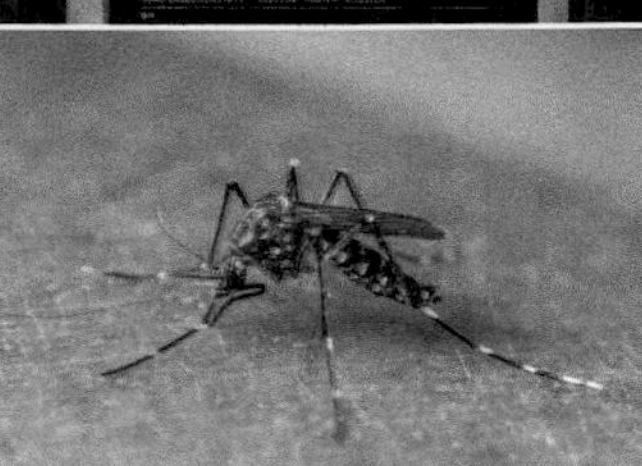

Synonyms
- connection

Antonyms
- irrelevance

Forms
- **Singular:** relevance
- **Plural:** relevance

Family
- **Adjective:** relevant

Word Partners
- direct/particular relevance
- personal relevance

Examples
- Earthquakes have **direct relevance** to people living in California.
- Classical music has **personal relevance** to me because I want to be an opera singer.

 **Try It**

____________ have particular **relevance** for people with allergies.

VERBAL PRACTICE

Talk about it — Discuss, Listen, Write

Discuss ideas with your partner, listen to classmates, and then write your favorite idea.

1. News reports about ____________ have little **relevance** for people living in ____________ .

2. The issue of ____________ is of particular **relevance** to me and my friends because we think about it almost everyday.

relevance

noun

WRITING PRACTICE

Collaborate
Discuss
Agree
Write
Listen

Discuss ideas with your partner and agree on the best words to complete the frame.

For many educators, ______________________________

has particular ______________ because they want their students to succeed.

Our Turn
Discuss
Listen
Write

Read the prompt. Work with the teacher to complete the frames. Write a thoughtful response that includes a relevant example.

PROMPT: Describe how elections for class officers on the student council have direct relevance to you and your classmates.

Student council elections have direct ______________ to me and my classmates

because class officers ______________________________. For example,

this year's candidates have promised to ______________________________

______________.

Be an Academic Author
Write
Discuss
Listen

Read the prompt and complete the frames. Strengthen your response with a convincing reason.

PROMPT: Describe an issue that seems to be of particular relevance to several adults that you know. Why do you think it is so important to them?

The issue of ______________________________ seems to be of particular

______________ to several adults that I know. One reason I think this is important is that

they ______________________________.

Construct a Response
Write
Discuss
Listen

Read the prompt and brainstorm ideas for a thoughtful response. Include a convincing reason to strengthen your response.

PROMPT: Many parents think that computer and video games have no direct relevance to their child's education. Describe some of the potential positive impacts of these games on a child's intellectual and social development.

____

____

____

grammar tip

Quantity adjectives tell "how much" or "how many." Quantity adjectives go before a plural noun. Common quantity adjectives are: *most, many, some, several, both.*

EXAMPLE: Most schools and **many** businesses were closed today because of the storm.

valid

adjective

***Say it:* val • id**

 ***Write it:*** ______________ ***Write it again:*** ______________

 ______________

TOOLKIT

Meaning

reasonable or sensible

Examples

- Joey gave a **valid** __________ for arriving late to class.

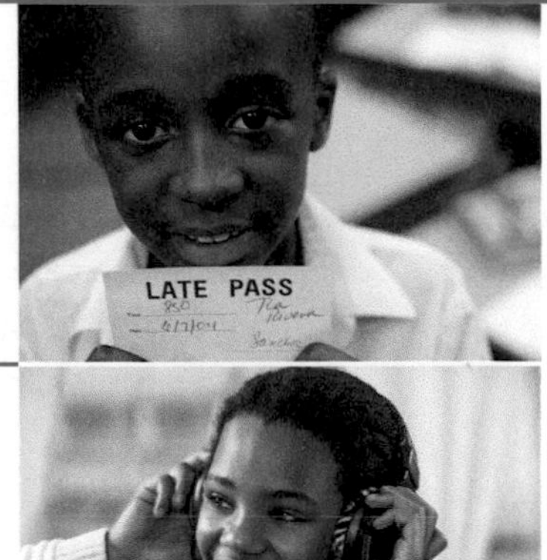

Synonyms

- reasonable

Antonyms

- invalid

- Since she was trying to win tickets to the __________, my sister had a **valid** reason for listening to the radio.

Family

- **Nouns:** validity; validation
- **Verb:** validate

Word Partners

- valid reason/argument
- valid point

Examples

- One **valid argument** for watching the news is to be informed about current events.
- I don't agree with you on this issue, but you have made a **valid point**.

 **Try It**

One **valid** reason for a failing grade is when a student doesn't ______________________________

______________.

VERBAL PRACTICE

Talk about it

Discuss
Listen
Write

Discuss ideas with your partner, listen to classmates, and then write your favorite idea.

1. ______________________________ isn't a **valid** excuse for being late.

2. One **valid** reason for wearing sunscreen is that it can protect you from

   ______________________.

valid

adjective

WRITING PRACTICE

Collaborate

Discuss
Agree
Write
Listen

Discuss ideas with your partner and agree on the best words to complete the frame.

One of many ______________ arguments for owning a cell phone is that it allows me to ______________________________.

Our Turn

Discuss
Listen
Write

Read the prompt. Work with the teacher to complete the frames. Write a thoughtful response that includes a personal experience and a relevant example.

PROMPT: Describe a time you assumed something about a person based on your first impression. Was it a valid assumption?

When I first met my ______________, I assumed (he/she) ________ would be very ______________. I thought this because (he/she) ________ seemed to ______________________. It turned out that this (was/was not) __________ a __________ assumption because (he/she) ________ is ______________.

Be an Academic Author

Write
Discuss
Listen

Read the prompt and complete the frames. Strengthen your response with a personal experience.

PROMPT: Describe a time when you exceeded someone's expectations. Were his/her expectations valid? How did it feel when you showed them what you were capable of doing?

Once, I exceeded my ______________ expectations when I ______________________________. It's clear that (his/her) __________ expectations (were/were not) __________ __________ because when I showed (him/her) __________ what I was capable of doing, it felt ______________________.

Construct a Response

Write
Discuss
Listen

Read the prompt and brainstorm ideas for a thoughtful response. Include convincing reasons to strengthen your response.

PROMPT: Many teachers would accept late work under special circumstances. Provide two valid reasons for receiving a three-day extension for a major U.S. history research report.

____

____

____

grammar tip

Adjectives are always singular even if they describe a plural noun. Do not add **-s** to adjectives that describe plural nouns.

EXAMPLE: My aunt is an **amazing** cook. She always makes **delicious** cakes and **delightful** pies.

point

SMARTSTART

REVIEW: interpretation *noun*

DAY 1

After our field trip to the art museum, we each had to present our

____________________ of one of the ____________________

that we had seen.

point *noun*

DAY 2

The main ____________________ of an article I recently read was that all

young children should be taught ____________________ in school.

DAY 3

The mayor made several good ____________________ in her argument

for expanding our public transportation services, including that it would

____ .

DAY 4

I convinced my family to go to the ____________________

last weekend by making the very valid ____________________ that each one

of us would find something interesting and enjoyable there.

DAY 5

I told my aunt I wanted to ____________________, but she

made the ____________________ that it was too dangerous.

TOTAL

SMARTSTART

REVIEW: point *noun*

DAY 1

Although I disagreed with my teacher about whether students should be able to ______________________________, I admit that (he/she) __________ made some valid ____________________ to support (his/her) __________ opinion.

emphasis *noun*

DAY 2

In order to lead happier lives, we should place more ____________________ on ______________________________ and less on stressful things like work and conflict.

DAY 3

When I want to put a special ____________________ on something I'm writing, I usually include ______________________________.

DAY 4

In the food we make at home, we place a lot of ____________________ on ____________________.

DAY 5

When you're learning how to ____________________, the instructors usually place a huge ____________________ on safety.

TOTAL

justify

SMART START

REVIEW: emphasis *noun*

DAY 1

Often, I think our news media place too much ____________________ on ____________________.

justify *verb*

DAY 2

We shouldn't try to ____________________ someone's ____________________ ____________________ behavior towards others.

DAY 3

I ____________________ not eating the ____________________ I was offered at my friend's house by saying that I had already eaten.

DAY 4

It's difficult to ____________________ spending a lot of money on ____________________ because they're simply not a necessity.

DAY 5

I feel that it is important for our country to ____________________ ____________________, and I can offer convincing evidence to ____________________ why I feel this way.

TOTAL

SMART START

REVIEW: justify *verb*

DAY 1

My brother tried to ______________ eating the last ______________, which was mine, by claiming there was nothing else to eat.

logical *adjective*

DAY 2

It is quite ______________ to make a copy of your ______________, just in case you lose it.

DAY 3

If you don't like ______________, then camping is probably not a ______________ choice of activity for you.

DAY 4

If you call your friend, but they don't answer the phone, one ______________ explanation is that ______________.

DAY 5

One ______________ argument for walking short distances rather than getting a ride is that it will be an excellent opportunity to ______________.

TOTAL

relevance

SMART START

REVIEW: logical *adjective*

DAY 1

If you enjoy big, exciting cities, then ______________________________ would be a

______________________________ choice for your next vacation.

relevance *noun*

DAY 2

When writing (a/an) __________ ______________________________ , you should only

include details that have direct ______________________________ to the topic.

DAY 3

Some people may think that historical events such as ______________________________

______________________________ have little ______________________________ for us

today, but I believe these events still affect our lives.

DAY 4

One song that has deep personal ______________________________ for me is

"____."

DAY 5

I especially enjoy learning about ______________________________ because I feel this has

direct ______________________________ to my future career.

TOTAL

SMART START

REVIEW: relevance *noun*

DAY 1

A paragraph about my personal food preferences would have little ______________ in a scientific essay about a healthy diet, but I could include information about ______________ ______________.

valid *adjective*

DAY 2

"______________" is definitely not a ______________ excuse for not completing a homework assignment.

DAY 3

One ______________ argument for abolishing homework for elementary school children is that ______________ ______________.

DAY 4

______________ is a ______________ way to get exercise without having to go to the gym.

DAY 5

A ______________ reason to wear a ______________ ______________ is that it will decrease your chances of being injured in an accident.

TOTAL

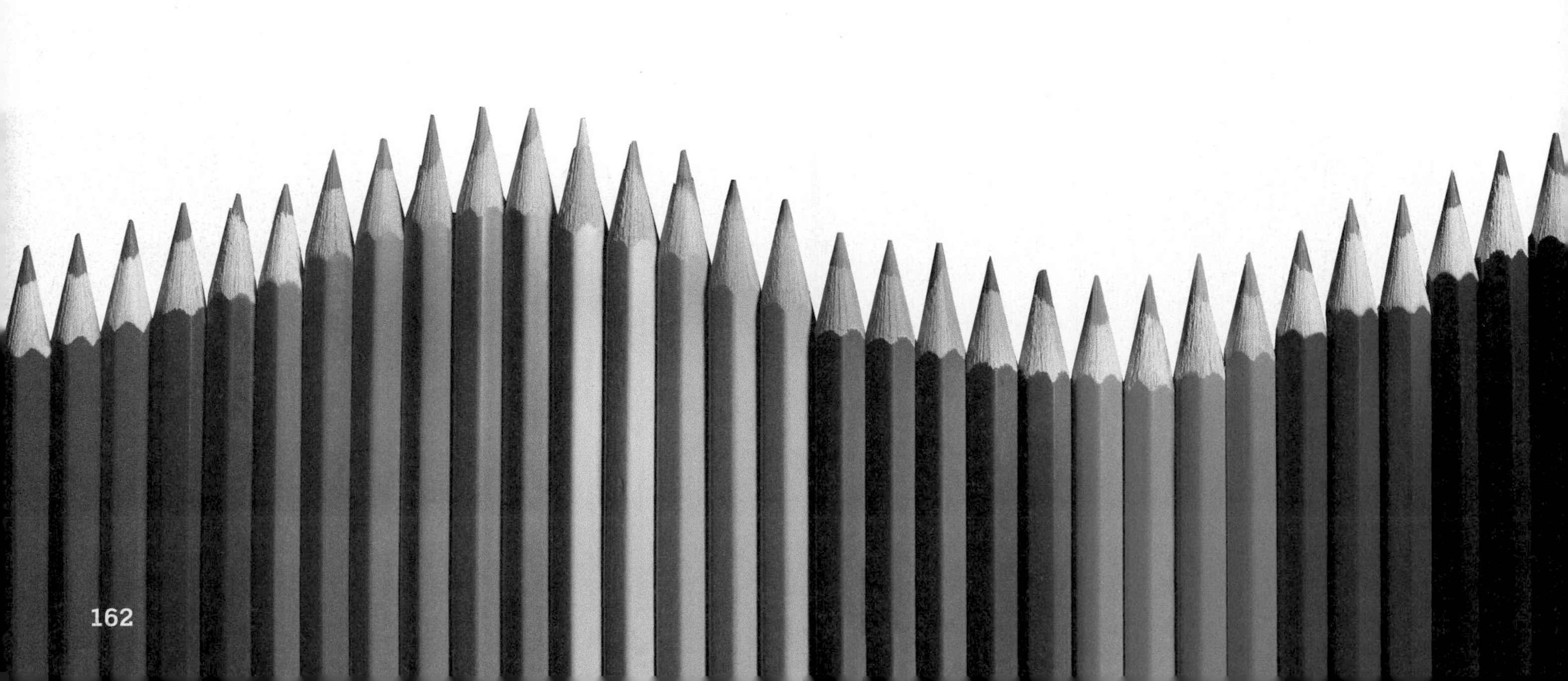

grammar lessons

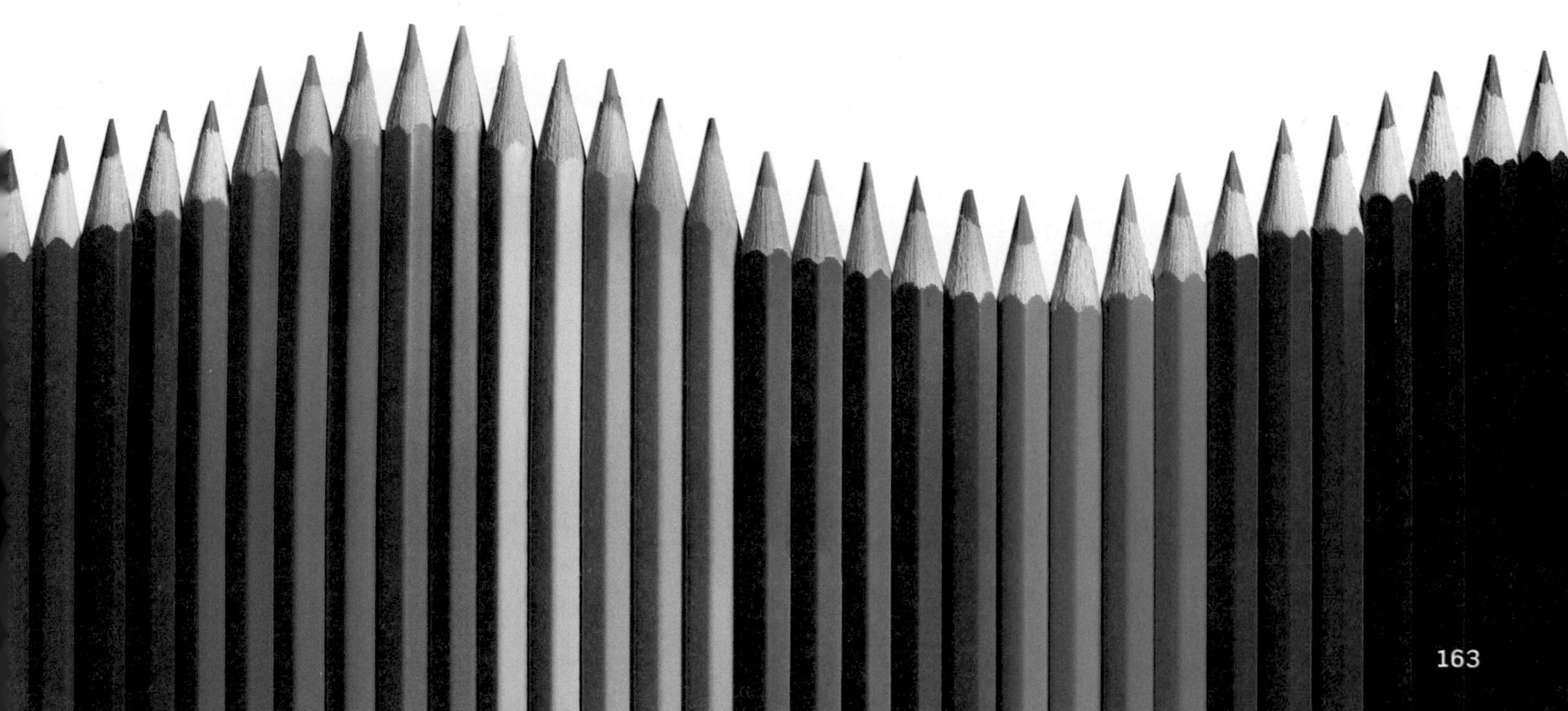

grammar

Present Tense Verbs

Use the present tense when you talk about actions that happen usually, sometimes, or regularly.

	Subject	Verb
Use the **base form** of the verb when the subject is *I, you, we,* or *they.*	I You We They	**edit** the essay. base form
Use the **-s** form of the verb when the subject is *he, she,* or *it.*	He She It	**edits** the essay. -s form

- When the base form of the verb ends in *s, sh, ch,* or *x,* add ***-es:*** ***miss*** → ***misses***; ***wash*** → ***washes***; ***catch*** → ***catches***; ***fix*** → ***fixes***
- When the base form of the verb ends in a consonant + *y,* change the *y* to *i* and add ***-es: cry*** → ***cries***

Find It

Read the sentences. Write the correct form of the present tense verb.

1. The morning of a test, Ella always (eat/eats) ________________ a healthy breakfast.
2. Some advertisements (exaggerate/exaggerates) ________________ the quality of the products they are selling.
3. The word "change" (mean/means) ________________ different things in different contexts.
4. My brother (try/tries) ________________ to get to school on time, but he often doesn't succeed!

Try It

Complete the sentences using the correct form of the verb.

1. Our teacher usually (provide) ________________ two different essay options.
2. Instead of drinking water, frogs (soak) ________________ it into their bodies through their skin.
3. Every year, we (watch) ________________ a video about lab safety before our first class in the lab.
4. The United States (elect) ________________ a president every four years.

Discuss and Write

Collaborate Discuss Agree Write Listen

Work with a partner. Use the correct form of the verbs to complete the sentences.

1. score/put — In basketball, players ______ a point when they ______ the ball through the basket.

2. discuss/read — My class ______ each chapter in our science textbook after we ______ it.

3. appear/represent — When an owl ______ in literature, it often ______ wisdom.

4. say/floss — My dentist ______ that I must ______ every day.

Your Turn Think Write

Work independently. Use the correct form of the verbs and your own words to complete the sentences.

1. make/add — When he ______ hot chocolate, he always ______ his special ingredient — ______!

2. imitate/see — Babies ______ many of the ______ they ______ adults make.

3. dig/hide — My dog often ______ holes in the backyard and then ______ a couple of ______ in it.

grammar

Adjectives and Adverbs

An *adjective* describes a noun.

An *adverb* describes a verb.

Adjective	Adverb
Alba is **polite**.	Alba speaks **politely** with adults.
We need **clear** directions.	The directions were not explained **clearly**.
The audience was **enthusiastic**.	The audience applauded **enthusiastically**.

- **An adjective usually comes before the noun it describes. An adjective can also come directly after the verb *be*: New York City is big.**
- **An adverb usually comes after the verb it describes. Most adverbs are formed by adding *-ly* to an adjective: *careful* → *carefully***

Find It

Complete the sentences with either the adjective or the adverb.

1. I reviewed the material (quick/quickly) ____________________ before the exam.
2. She was so (angry/angrily) ____________________ that she had to take a few breaths to calm down.
3. We watched a (brief/briefly) ____________________ video about climate change.
4. Jack arranged the papers (neat/neatly) ____________________ in two piles.

Try It

Complete the sentences using the correct form (adjective or adverb) of the word.

1. My little sister was proud that she could tie her shoes (independent) ____________________.
2. It's a (fascinating) ____________________ article because it gives the reader new insights into the issue.
3. The jury looked (close) ____________________ at the evidence.
4. I prefer the (original) ____________________version of that song.

Discuss and Write

Collaborate Discuss Agree Write Listen

Work with a partner. Write the sentence, including the adverb or adjective provided.

1. (awkward) There were many pauses in the mayor's speech.

   ____

   ____

2. (convince) She spoke about the need for more study hall periods.

   ____

   ____

3. (serious) My parents and I had a discussion about my grades.

   ____

   ____

Your Turn Think Write

Work independently. Use the correct form of the word (adjective or adverb) and your own words to complete the sentences.

1. (complete) The scientific concept of ____________ is difficult to understand ____________.
2. (prompt) If you don't arrive for your doctor's appointment ____________, you may have to ____________.
3. (nervous) He was ____________ about ____________ on his own for the first time
4. (interesting) I think the most ____________ TV channels are the ones that focus on the topic of ____________.

grammar

Adverbs of Frequency

Use adverbs of frequency to talk about how often actions happen.

	Adverbs of Frequency	Examples with the Verb *Be*	Examples with Other Verbs
100%	always	My mother **is always** in bed by 9:00.	She **always goes** to bed by 9:00.
↑	usually	I **am usually** in the library on Tuesday afternoons.	I **usually go** to the library on Tuesday afternoons.
	often	They **are often** busy on the weekend.	They **often have** plans on the weekend.
	sometimes	My brother **is sometimes** impatient.	He **sometimes shows** impatience.
↓	rarely	She **is rarely** late to school.	She **rarely comes** to school late.
0%	never	It **is never** hot in Antarctica.	It **never gets** hot in Antarctica.

- Put adverbs of frequency after the verb *be*.
- Put adverbs of frequency before all other verbs.

Find It

Read the pairs of sentences. Underline the sentence that has the adverb of frequency in the right place.

1. I read usually before I got to sleep. | I usually read before I go to sleep.
2. The dog always barks at the mail carrier. | The dog barks always at the mail carrier.
3. Mr. Diaz never is in a bad mood. | Mr. Diaz is never in a bad mood.
4. Little children are rarely patient. | Rarely are little children patient.

Try It

Write the sentences and include the adverb of frequency. Be sure to put it in the correct place.

1. (usually) Laurel is the first student on the bus in the morning.

____

2. (always) Lightning comes before thunder.

____

3. (often) I change my password to keep my account secure.

____

4. (rarely) My brother wakes up before noon on Saturday.

____

Discuss and Write

Collaborate Discuss Agree Write Listen

Work with a partner. Complete the sentences using appropriate adverbs of frequency and your own words.

1. Science textbooks ______________ illustrate difficult concepts with (a/an) ________ ______________.
2. The graduating class ______________ takes a trip to ______________. It's become a school tradition!
3. She ______________ reads novels because she prefers ______________.
4. Not getting enough sleep ______________ results in feeling ______________ the next day.

Your Turn Think Write

Work independently. Complete the sentences using appropriate adverbs of frequency and your own words.

1. I don't know why, but my brother and I ______________ argue over ______________ things.
2. He ______________ eats meat, but every once in awhile he gets a craving for a ______________.
3. Consuming too much sugar ______________ leads to developing health problems such as ______________.
4. I look for (a/an) ________ ______________ whenever I go to the beach, but so far, I've ______________ found one.

grammar

Present Progressive Tense

Use the present progressive to talk about an action that is happening right now.

Subject	*be*	Verb + *-ing*
I	**am**	
He She It	**is**	listen**ing** to a podcast.
You We They	**are**	

- To form the progressive tense of most verbs, and ***-ing*** to the base form of the verb: read → ***reading***
- For verbs that end in a consonant + ***–e***, drop the ***–e*** before adding ***-ing***: dance → ***dancing***

Find It

Complete the sentences using the correct form of the verb.

1. My class is (collect) ______________________ money for a children's charity.

2. Something is (burn) ______________________ in the oven!

3. The television is (distract) ______________________ me from focusing on my homework.

4. We're (wait) ______________________ to hear the results of the election.

Try It

Read the present tense sentences. Write the sentences as present progressive sentences.

1. The baby looks at himself in the mirror.

   ____

2. I gather information for my essay.

   ____

3. Tilo auditions for the lead role in the school play.

   ____

4. The farmers harvest their crops.

   ____

Discuss and Write

Collaborate Discuss Agree Write Listen

Work with a partner. Use the correct form of the verbs to complete the sentences.

1. pose/take — The actress is ______________ while the photographers are ______________ her picture.

2. try/feel — I am __trying__ to finish my homework, but I am __feeling__ very sleepy.

3. watch/take — We are __watching__ a video and __taking__ notes on important details.

Your Turn Think Write

Work independently. Use the correct form of the verb and your own words to complete the sentences.

1. search — We are __searching__ all over the house for the __wallet__ that my sister lost this morning.

2. research — Scientists are __investigate__ ways to __research a new antidote__.

3. interview — The reporter is __interviewing__ the man who witnessed the __accident__.

4. save — I'm __saving__ my babysitting money to buy __a new car__.

grammar

Past Tense Verbs

Use the past tense to talk about events or actions that have already happened.

Subject	Base Form of Verb + *-ed/-d*	
I He She It You We They	suggest**ed**	some essay topics.

- To form the simple past tense of most regular verbs, add ***-ed*** to the base form of the verb: ***listen* ➝ *listened***
- For regular verbs that end in *-e*, add ***-d***: ***smile* ➝ *smiled***

Find It

Read the sentences. Write the correct form of the verb.

1. He accidentally (deletes/deleted) ______________ a paragraph from his essay last night.
2. Water (boils/boiled) ______________ at 212 degrees Fahrenheit.
3. The delivery person (deliver/delivered) ______________ the package to the wrong house, so I never received it.
4. My teacher generally (emphasizes/emphasized) ___________ the importance of providing evidence.

Try It

Complete the sentences using the correct form of the verb.

1. My two favorite songwriters (collaborate) ______________ on this song last year.
2. The accident was so long ago that it's difficult to remember the sequence in which the events (happen) ______________ .
3. I sent you a text message, but you never (respond) ______________ .
4. This morning we (analyze) ______________ the motive of the main characters in the novel.

Discuss and Write

Collaborate Discuss Agree Write Listen

Work with a partner. Use the correct form of the verbs to complete the sentences.

1. explode/cook — The other day, an egg ______________ when I ______________ it in the microwave.

2. discover/land — Newton ______________ gravity when an apple ______________ on his head.

3. compare/contrast — Yesterday in social studies class, we ______________ and ______________ the American and the French revolutions.

Your Turn Think Write

Work independently. Use the correct form of the verbs and your own words to complete the sentences.

1. taste/measure — The lemonade we made yesterday ______________ incredibly ______________ because we ______________ the ingredients incorrectly.

2. check/correct — I ______________ my report and ______________ all of the ______________ errors before I printed it out.

3. knock/shatter — When Tim ______________ the ______________ vase off the table, it ______________ into dozens of pieces.

4. laugh/pull — The little boy ______________ when the clown ______________ (a/an) ________ ______________ out of his ear.

grammar

Possessive Nouns

Use **possessive nouns** to show that something belongs to someone or something.

	Singular Noun	Possessive Noun	Example
To show that something belongs to someone or something, add an apostrophe (') and **-s** at the end of a singular noun.	computer	computer**'s**	The computer**'s** screen is locked.

	Plural Noun that ends in -s	Possessive Noun	Example
To show that something belongs to more than one person or thing, add an apostrophe (') at the end of a plural noun, following the -s.	computers	computers**'**	All of the computer**s'** screens are locked.

Find It

Complete the sentences using the correct possessive noun.

1. A (word's/words') ______________________ context can help reveal its meaning.

2. I take care of my (neighbor's/neighbors') ____________ pets whenever they go out of town.

3. The (house's/houses') ______________________ roof was damaged in the storm.

4. People are often surprised to learn that (polar bear's/polar bears') ______________________ skin is black.

Try It

Complete the sentences with the correct possessive form of the noun.

1. The little (boy) ______________________ ice-cream cone is dripping.

2. All of our (cellphones) ______________________ ringers have the same sound, so we never know which of us is getting a call!

3. The counselors set up all of the (campers) ______________________ tents by the lake.

4. The (building) ______________________ security code is changed each week.

Discuss and Write

Collaborate — Discuss, Agree, Write, Listen

Work with a partner. Read the first sentence. Then complete the second sentence with the correct possessive noun.

1. The handwriting of the doctor is difficult to read.

   The ________________ handwriting is difficult to read.

2. The humps of camels store fat.

   ________________ humps store fat.

3. The wheels of all of the bicycles are deflated.

   All of the ________________ wheels are deflated.

4. The frosting of the cake is homemade.

   The ________________ frosting is homemade.

Your Turn — Think, Write

Work independently. Complete the sentences with the correct possessive form of the noun and your own words.

1. (author) This ________________ writing style is very ____________________.

2. (cars) There was a manufacturing problem at the factory. All of the ________________ airbags seem to be ____________________.

3. (flashlight) The ________________ batteries are ____________________.

4. (students) Some of the ________________ biographies include information about their ________________________________.

grammar

There, Their, They're

There, their, and they're are homophones. Homophones are words that have the same sound, but are spelled differently and have different meanings.

Word	Explanation	Example
there	*There* is an adverb that means *that place.* *There* is also used with the verb *be* to introduce a sentence or clause.	Wait for me. I'll be **there** in 10 minutes. **There** are 100 senators in Congress.
their	*Their* shows ownership. It is always followed by a noun.	I asked them to bring **their** guitars tonight.
they're	*They're* is a contraction formed by putting together the words *they* + *are.*	**They're** applying to the same college.

Find It

Read the sentences. Choose the correct word to complete the sentences.

1. Ella and Jonah have been in school together since kindergarten, so (their/they're) ________________ very sad about going to different high schools next year.

2. John and Alex couldn't get on the train because they lost (their/they're) ________________ tickets.

3. We're going to be sitting right over (there/they're) ________________ during the concert.

4. My teacher always says that (there/their) ________________ are no excuses for sloppy work.

Try It

Complete the sentences using *there*, *their*, or *they're*.

1. I forgot my lunch today, so my friends shared ________________ lunches with me.

2. ________________ are seven continents on Earth.

3. Where did they park ________________ car?

4. I only bought these shoes a few months ago, but ________________ already out of fashion.

Discuss and Write

Collaborate Discuss Agree Write Listen

Work with a partner. Complete the sentences using *there, their,* and *they're*.

1. ______________________ trying to think of a topic for ________________ group project.

2. The construction workers left ______________________ tools over ______________________ .

3. ______________________ are three people with the name Emma in the seventh grade and ______________________ all in my homeroom!

Your Turn Think Write

Work independently. Complete the sentences with *there, their,* and *they're* and your own words.

1. ______________________ home was damaged by the ______________________ .

2. I think the reason ______________________ are so many cars parked on the street is that there is a __________________________________ happening down the road.

3. I don't want to go to the ______________________ because I was just ______________________ a few days ago.

4. Most parents teach ______________________ children not to ______________________ .

grammar

▶ Modal Verbs

A **modal verb** is a helping verb that adds more meaning to the main verb.

Example Sentence	Subject	Modal	Base Form of Verb		Meaning
She **could** win the election.	She	**could**	win	the election.	Use *could* to show that something might be possible.
You **should** stop worrying so much.	You	**should**	stop	worrying so much.	Use *should* to make suggestions or recommendations.
I **would** buy a pizza if I had money.	I	**would**	buy	a pizza if I had money.	Use *would* to show that something is possible under certain conditions.

Find It

Read the sentences. Complete the sentences with the best modal choice.

1. She's so tired that she (could/should) ____________ probably fall asleep standing up!
2. You (should/would) ____________ consider both sides of an argument carefully before deciding.
3. We (would/could) ____________ work on the project together.
4. It (would/should) ____________ be difficult to heat food quickly without a microwave.

Try It

Complete the sentences with the correct modal + verb forms.

1. You (should spend/would spend) ____________ less time taking selfies.
2. She (would get/would gets) ____________ her ears pierced, but she's afraid it will hurt.
3. We (could save/should save) ____________ 10% if we enrolled for membership cards.

Discuss and Write

Collaborate
Discuss
Agree
Write
Listen

Work with a partner. Complete the sentences with the best modal choices. Use the modals *could*, *should*, and *would*.

1. You ______________________________ donate those toys to a charity since someone else ______________________________ use them.

2. We ______________________________ boil the carrots, but then they ______________________________ lose all of their flavor.

3. I ______________________________ look up the word in the dictionary, but my teacher says I ______________________________ try to figure out the meaning of a word from its context first.

4. If you see lightning, it ______________________________ be dangerous, so you ______________________________ go inside the house.

Your Turn
Think
Write

Work independently. Choose the best modal and your own words to complete the sentences. Use the modals *could*, *should*, and *would*.

1. He ________________________ train his dog not to ______________________________ .

2. Without bees to pollinate plants, we ______________________________ not have many ______________________________ to eat.

3. You ______________________________ make sure to ______________________________ your sprained ankle.

4. If we lived near the ______________________________ we ______________________________ go there all the time!

Acknowledgments, continued from page ii

vi (tl) ©Don Tran/Shutterstock.com. (tr) ©Fuse/Corbis/Getty Images. (cl) ©Dragon Images/Shutterstock.com. (br) ©Fuse/Corbis/Getty Images. **viii** (tl) ©Jupiterimages/Stockbyte/Getty Images. (tr) ©HomeArt/Shutterstock.com. (cl) ©Andre Goncalves/Shutterstock.com. (br) ©Chris Schmidt/E+/Getty Images.
x (tl) ©Peeradach Rattanakoses/ShutterStock.com. (tr) ©Robert Daly/OJO Images/Getty Images. (cl) ©Mike Flippo/Shutterstock.com. (br) ©Milica Nistoran/Shutterstock.com. **2** ERproductions Ltd/Blend Images/Getty Images. **4** (cr) ©Nickolay Vinokurov/Shutterstock.com. (tr) ©wavebreakmedia/Shutterstock.com. **6** (tr) ©ImagesBazaar/Getty Images. (cr) ©grafvision/Shutterstock.com. **8** (tr) ©Yegor Larin/Shutterstock.com. (cr) ©Martin Novak/Shutterstock.com. **10** (cr) ©Fotos593/Shutterstock.com. (tr) ©koya979/Shutterstock.com. **12** (tr) ©Christopher Futcher/Getty Images. (cr) ©Dusan Zidar/Shutterstock.com. **14** (cr) ©Dean Drobot/Shutterstock.com. (tr) ©monkeybusinessimages/Getty Images.
22 (cl) Shchipkova Elena/Shutterstock.com. (tr) Vadim Sadovski/Shutterstock.com. **24** (cr) ©Gayvoronskaya_Yana/Shutterstock.com. (tr) ©Ariel Skelley/Blend Images/Getty Images.
26 (cr) ©Reinhard Dirscherl/WaterFrame/Getty Images. (tr) ©Todd Gipstein/ National Geographic Creative. **28** (tr) ©Matthew Ennis/Shutterstock.com. (cr) ©Junial Enterprises/Shutterstock.com. **30** (tr) ©Piotr Marcinski/Shutterstock.com. (cr) ©racorn/Shutterstock.com. **32** (tr) ©Andersen Ross/Blend Images/Getty Images. (cr) ©KidStock/Getty Images.
34 (cr) ©monticello/Shutterstock.com. (tr) ©PeopleImages.com/DigitalVision/Getty Images. **42** Lopolo/Shutterstock.com.
44 (tr1) Sarah Holmlund/Shutterstock.com. (tr2) Don Tran/Shutterstock.com. **46** (tr1) Wavebreakmedia/Shutterstock.com. (tr2) Wong sze yuen/Shutterstock.com. **48** (tr1) Shah Rohani/Shutterstock.com. (tr2) Kali9/E+/Getty Images. **50** (tr1) Guas/Shutterstock.com. (tr2) Tom Wang/Shutterstock.com.
52 (tr1) 9peaks/Shutterstock.com. (tr2) Fuse/Corbis/Getty Images. **54** (tr1) JGI/Tom Grill/Blend Images/Getty Images. (tr2) Will & Deni McIntyre/Corbis Documentary/Getty Images.
62 Alena Brozova/Shutterstock.com. **64** (tr1) Mike Watson Images/Moodboard/Getty Images. (tr2) Jade/Blend Images/Getty Images.
66 (tr1) Randy Duchaine/Alamy Stock Photo. (tr2) Dragon Images/Shutterstock.com. **68** (tr1) Duplass/Shutterstock.com. (tr2) Fuse/Corbis/Getty Images. **70** (tr1) Bioraven/Shutterstock.com. (tr2) Chris Clinton/The Image Bank/Getty Images. **72** (tr1) Michael Steele/Getty Images Sport/Getty Images. (tr2) BlueOrange Studio/Shutterstock.com. **74** (tr1) Namart Pieamsuwan/Shutterstock.com. (tr2) Roger Ressmeyer/Corbis/VCG/Getty Images. **82** Sergey Novikov/Shutterstock.com. **84** (tr1) YanLev/Shutterstock.com. (tr2) Library of Congress Prints and Photographs Division Washington [LC-DIG-ppmsca-47032]. **86** (tr1) Greg Vote/Tetra images/Getty Images. (tr2) KidStock/Blend Images/Getty Images. **88** (tr1) Pjcross/Shutterstock.com. (tr2) NoBorders - Brayden Howie/Shutterstock.com. **90** (tr1) Tracy A. Woodward/The Washington Post/Getty Images. (tr2) Blend Images/Hill Street Studios/Alamy Stock Photo. **92** (tr1) Tyler Olson/Shutterstock.com. (tr2) Jupiterimages/Exactostock-1557/Superstock. **94** (tr1) Jupiterimages/Stockbyte/Getty Images. (tr2) HomeArt/Shutterstock.com.
102 Michael Pettigrew/Shutterstock.com.
104 (tr1) Ken Canning/Vetta/Getty Images. (tr2) The Asahi Shimbun/Getty Images.
106 (tr1) Africa Studio/Shutterstock.com. (tr2) Phil Boorman/Cultura/Getty Images. **108** (tr1) WPA Pool/Getty Images News/Getty Images. (tr2) Monkey Business Images/Shutterstock.com. **110** (tr1) Andre Goncalves/Shutterstock.com. (tr2) Arka38/Shutterstock.com. **112** (tr1) Andrew Burton/Getty Images News/Getty Images. (tr2) Kenzo Tribouillard/AFP/Getty Images. **114** (tr1) Joseph Sohm/Shutterstock.com. (tr2) Chris Schmidt/E+/Getty Images.
122 Syaheir Azizan/Shutterstock.com. **124** (tr1) DGLimages/Shutterstock.com. (tr2) Michael Kelley/The Image Bank/Getty Images. **126** (tr1) Peeradach Rattanakoses/Shutterstock.com. (tr2) Boris-B/Shutterstock.com. **128** (tr1) Jeafish Ping/Shutterstock.com. (tr2) Ollyy/Shutterstock.com. **130** (tr1) Image Source/Getty Images. (tr2) Paul Ekert/Shutterstock.com. **132** (tr1) Clive Rose/Getty Images Sport/Getty Images. (tr2) Burlingham/Shutterstock.com. **134** (tr1) Robert Daly/OJO Images/Getty Images. (tr2) PhotoAlto/Frederic Cirou/Getty Images.
142 Monkey Business Images/Shutterstock.com.
144 (tr1) Tazzymoto/Shutterstock.com. (tr2) Monkeybusinessimages/iStock/Getty Images.
146 (tr1) Elena Vasilchenko/Shutterstock.com. (tr2) Steve Debenport/E+/Getty Images.
148 (tr1) Mimagephotography/Shutterstock.com. (tr2) Panya Kuanun/Shutterstock.com.
150 (tr1) Stefano Cavoretto/Shutterstock.com. (tr2) Mike Flippo/Shutterstock.com. **152** (tr1) Bplanet/Shutterstock.com. (tr2) Smith1972/Shutterstock.com. **154** (tr1) Creatas/Getty Images Plus/Getty Images. (tr2) Milica Nistoran/Shutterstock.com.